The Palliative Care Handbook

Guidelines for clinical management and symptom control

This edition by Rod MacLeod and Steve Macfarlane has been revised and adapted to include the care of people with dementia and is based on previous editions written by Rod MacLeod, Jane Vella-Brincat and Sandy Macleod.

Prof Rod MacLeod
Senior Consultant in Palliative Care,
HammondCare
Honorary Professor in the Sydney Medical
School (Northern), University of Sydney

Dr Steve Macfarlane
Geriatric Psychiatrist
Head of Clinical Services,
The Dementia Centre
HammondCare, Sydney

HammondCare
Media

Published by HammondCare Media - Ninth edition - 2018
Sydney Australia
hammondcaremedia@hammond.com.au
ISBN: 978-0-6482415-7-7

Cover design and typesetting: Kylie Mulquin. Printed in Australia by SOS print + media

National Library of Australia Cataloguing-in-Publication data:

NATIONAL LIBRARY OF AUSTRALIA

A catalogue record for this book is available from the National Library of Australia

Acknowledgements

We are grateful to HammondCare for funding the printing of this edition.
The organ failure at the end-of-life section and much of the drug interaction data is based on part of the Canterbury District Health Board's Preferred Medicines List, Antimicrobial Guidelines and Pharmacology Guidelines 19th Ed. 2015

Thanks to Dr Helen Lunt for the diabetes section, Dr Elaine Rogers for the cachexia section and Dr Richard Egan for input into the spirituality section. Nutrition in palliative care is written by Melissa Scattergood, Clinical Dietitian and the section on deprescribing by Andriana Colic, Clinical Oncology Pharmacist – Royal North Shore Hospital, Sydney. We are grateful to all for their expertise and to other colleagues at HammondCare who have made helpful suggestions for improvements.

Many of the medications listed are being used outside their product licence. Prescription of a drug (whether licensed use/route or not) requires the prescriber, in the light of published evidence, to balance both the potential good and the potential harm which might ensue. Prescribers have a duty to act with reasonable care and skill in a manner consistent with the practice of professional colleagues of similar standing. Thus, when prescribing outside the terms of the licence, prescribers must be fully informed about the actions and uses of the drug, and be assured of the quality of the particular product (www.palliativedrugs.com/ using-licensed-drugs-for-unlicensed-purposes). Prescribers also have a duty to inform patients that drugs are being used outside their licence and to inform them of any expected effects and side effects. Care has been taken to ensure accuracy of information at time of printing. This information may change and final responsibility lies with the prescriber. Some medication will incur a cost to the user, it is important to consider this before prescribing

This Handbook should be used in conjunction with Therapeutic Guidelines – Palliative Care – version 3 (Therapeutic Guidelines Limited, Melbourne) where possible

Throughout the book, drugs that are either not available or not funded in New Zealand are marked with *

Abbreviations

subcut	subcutaneous	CNS	central nervous system
bd	twice daily	LFTs	liver function tests
tds	three times daily	MAOIs	monoamine oxidase inhibitors
qid	four times daily	NSAIDs	nonsteroidal anti-inflammatory drugs

Foreword

Palliative care has come a long way from the beginnings of the modern hospice movement in the 1960s and is now widely understood as an essential part of care for the whole person during life-limiting illness and at end-of-life.

Increasingly we are aware of the importance of being able to provide palliative care when and where it is needed and this often means involving palliative care earlier in the course of illness and not just in hospital or hospice, but at home and in residential care.

Alongside these developments, dementia has become a leading cause of death in many nations, something which is still relatively new to our experience, but which can be expected to increase.

As a result, the interaction of palliative care with the end-of-life needs of a person with dementia has never been more important or prevalent and yet this is not widely addressed in literature and clinical support.

As the authors of *The Palliative Care Handbook* (ninth edition) point out, too often people with dementia miss out on palliative care referrals and treatments that could make such a difference for them in their final days.

Which is why this new edition is so vital. Not only have the highly regarded clinical and pharmacological guidelines been fully updated, extensive notes and advice have been included for the first time specifically addressing the end-of-life needs of people with dementia.

To accomplish this, original author, Prof Rod MacLeod and new author, Dr Stephen Macfarlane, have used their extensive expertise and experience to add many important insights and guidelines for palliative care in the context of dementia.

There is no doubt that this new edition of *The Palliative Care Handbook* will continue to support excellence in palliative care around the world and now also support a growing awareness of the palliative needs of people with dementia.

A/Prof Colm Cunningham
Director of the Dementia Centre
HammondCare

Contents

Introduction

Welcome to the ninth edition of *The Palliative Care Handbook.* This edition has been extensively revised and for the first time includes specific guidelines to inform management of the provision of palliative care services to those living with dementia.

Dementia is now the leading cause of death for women in Australia (second leading cause overall) and a number of other Western countries. Yet the rates of referral of those with dementia to palliative care or hospice services remain very low, with most dying either in hospital wards or in aged care homes. Even when it has been recognised that a person with dementia has entered the dying phase, those with dementia are significantly less likely to receive palliative medications, including analgesia.

It is unclear whether this data reflects a lack of comfort that palliative care professionals have in working with people with dementia, or ignorance around the issues that those dying with dementia might face – research in the area is sorely lacking. What is known, however, is that the health needs at the end-of-life for those with dementia are comparable to the needs of those dying from cancer.

Part of the problem may lie in the difficulties health professionals experience in determining the prognosis of a person with dementia. The average duration between the diagnosis of dementia and dying from dementia is around 10 years, and even people with advanced dementia might, by the time they enter this stage of illness, survive another 2 or 3 years. In one study, only 1.1% of residents with advanced dementia were perceived to have a life expectancy of 6 months or less, yet 71% died within this time. A failure to recognise the onset of the dying process in a person with dementia exposes them to unnecessary investigations, hospital admissions, medical procedures and prescription of psychotropic drugs, whilst depriving them of more appropriate palliative interventions.

Regardless of the low rates of referral to palliative care of those with a primary diagnosis of dementia it is undeniable that, as the population ages, palliative care services will increasingly encounter patients for whom dementia is a significant comorbidity that will impact upon their management in a palliative care setting.

It is timely, then, for issues related to dementia to assume a greater importance within the palliative care sphere. It is hoped that this edition of *The Palliative Care Handbook* might be a step towards this.

The first section of this book is a set of guidelines for the alleviation of symptoms commonly encountered in palliative care. Drug therapy is included.

The second section (the pharmacopoeia) contains drug information:

- It is in alphabetical order by generic drug name.
- The interactions listed include discussion about enzymes responsible for drug metabolism commonly known as Cytochrome P450 (CYP) enzymes. There are many CYP enzymes some of which are genetically controlled. The interactions listed are based mainly on theory, are subject to change as more is learnt about the CYP enzyme system and are meant to be used as a guide only to potential interactions. Only commonly used palliative care drugs have been included but interactions with other drugs may also occur.
- There is also information about the use of syringe drivers.

While drug information in this book relates primarily to availability in Australia and New Zealand, the medications will generally be available in the UK, US and internationally. Where needed, further information is available from your nation's regulatory agency e.g. the UK Medicines and Healthcare Products Regulatory Agency and the US Food and Drug Administration.

Palliative care aims

- to achieve the best possible quality of life for patients and their families
- to understand and address patients' physical, psychological, social and spiritual suffering
- to be applicable from early on in the course of the illness

The World Health Organisation defines palliative care as:

'An approach that improves the quality of life of patients and their families facing the problems associated with a life-threatening illness, through the prevention and relief of suffering by means of early identification and impeccable assessment and treatment of pain and other problems, physical, psychosocial and spiritual.'

Palliative care:

- provides relief from pain and other distressing symptoms
- affirms life and regards dying as a normal process
- intends neither to hasten or postpone death
- integrates the psychological and spiritual aspects of patient care
- provides support to help patients live as actively as possible
- provides support to the family during the illness and bereavement
- uses a multidisciplinary team approach
- enhances quality of life and influences the course of the illness
- is applicable early in the course of illness alongside therapies that are intended to prolong life (e.g. chemotherapy, radiotherapy) and diagnostic investigations

General symptom management principles

- accurate and meticulous assessment is essential
- assess and address non-physical as well as physical issues
- difficult to control symptoms may require several different approaches
- aim for highest possible quality of life
- use risk versus benefit assessments when side effects of therapy occur
- explain issues as much as possible to the patient and their carers
- use a multidisciplinary approach
- reassess continuously

Central nervous system

Dementia

Dementia is an insidious, global deterioration of cognition without impairment of consciousness. More than 100 causes are recognised, though most of these are exceedingly rare:

- a terminal disease (albeit slow) with a median survival of 7 to 10 years post-diagnosis
- prevalence of 10% in over 65-year-olds, 20% in over 80-year-olds, 40% in 90-year-olds, and for indigenous Australians the prevalence is 3 to 5 times that of non-indigenous Australians
- About 1% of all dementia is considered early-onset (age < 65). In indigenous Australians, early-onset disease is defined by an age of onset <50 years

Types

- Alzheimer's is the most common (70% of all dementias)
  - predominant early deficits are episodic memory and orientation to time.
- vascular (30% of all dementias)
  - accompanies a history of cardiovascular events (CVA/TIA)
  - islets of retained functioning
  - language is preserved
  - dysexecutive syndrome
  - gait disturbance
  - subcortical signs
- frontotemporal (FTD – 10% of all dementias; commonest cause of early-onset disease)
  - can occur in those with Motor Neurone Disease (10 to 15%)
  - disinhibition, apathy and loss of empathy
  - hyperorality, lability, poor insight and compulsive, perseverative behaviours
- Lewy body dementia (LBD)
  - Parkinsonism
  - visual hallucinations and cognitive fluctuations
  - cognitive fluctuations typically marked
  - REM-Sleep behaviour disorder
  - vulnerability to delirium
  - extreme sensitivity to antipsychotics – quetiapine is the agent of choice.
- treatable causes
  - depressive pseudodementia
  - subdural and hypothyroidism
  - B_{12}/folate deficiency
  - syphilis

- others
  - Parkinson's disease (essentially very similar to Lewy body dementia), Huntington's, alcoholic, post traumatic brain injury, paraneoplastic, post encephalitic

Note that mixed types of dementia become increasingly common with age, and that end-stage dementia (regardless of cause) tends to assume a common phenotype. With the exception of Lewy body dementia, determining the exact type of dementia in a palliative/end-stage setting is much less important than recognition and appropriate treatment of a behavioural syndrome.

Assessment

- Take an extensive history (in end-stage dementia this will invariably need to be from a family member or close caregiver).
- Formally assess mental state, including the use of cognitive screening tools e.g. Mini-Mental State Examination (MMSE), Montreal Cognitive Assessment (MoCA) - where the patient retains verbal skills. (see 'Useful resources' p. 162)
- In many cases a formal cognitive evaluation will not be possible in advanced dementia, but the broader mental status examination remains invaluable, particularly in relation to:
  - General appearance and behaviour. Is the patient agitated, distressed, vocalising? Are there any signs of drug side effects (Parkinsonian facies, resting tremor, dyskinetic movements - oro-lingual dyskinesias are particularly common), dystonic reactions, motor tics or perseveration?
  - Affect - does the patient's expression reflect sadness, anxiety, anger? Are they guarded and suspicious? Lability may reflect frontal involvement, and should be differentiated from depression.
  - Perception. Does the person appear to be responding to external stimuli?

Behavioural and Psychological Symptoms of Dementia (BPSD)

- delirium
  - a careful history is vital. The biggest single risk factor for delirium is the presence of pre-existing cognitive impairment, so those with dementia are at vastly increased risk. Reduced cognitive reserve lowers delirium threshold.
  - A history of acute deterioration (cognitive, functional, behavioural) in the setting of previously stable impairments should always suggest delirium, and should be treated as such.
- depression (treat early initially with a SSRI or mirtazapine)
  - this is a difficult diagnosis to make in the presence of advanced dementia, where the patient's ability to report symptoms accurately is compromised
  - clinicians are advised to fall back on the presence of 'hard-core' biological symptoms of depression in this setting (recent change in sleep or appetite patterns, complete anhedonia, self-harm behaviour)
  - if there is any doubt, erring on the side of a trial of treatment is often advisable. Depression should be on the list of differential diagnoses for most behavioural disturbances in dementia, and modern antidepressants are much less toxic than the antipsychotic drugs that might otherwise be prescribed

- Mirtazapine is a useful drug in this patient group. It has beneficial effects on sleep, appetite and anxiety that occur early in the course of treatment and which are independent of its antidepressant effects
- The minimum antidepressant dose of mirtazapine is 30mg. If treating depression there is generally no advantage to commencing at a lower dose (often justified on the basis of minimising sedation…mirtazapine is an inverse agonist at the histamine receptor, however, and thus is more sedating at lower doses)

- agitation/aggression (consider low dose short term antipsychotics, benzodiazepines)
  - identify precipitants (can be difficult)
  - avoid confrontation
  - if the issue is agitation alone, antipsychotics hold no advantage over benzodiazepines, and are considerably more toxic
  - an intermediate half-life benzodiazepine with no active metabolites (e.g. oxazepam 7.5-15mg, temazepam 10mg) is the safest choice
  - there is evidence for the use of low-dose risperidone in the management of aggression, but the effect size is small (~0.2)
- anxiety
  - peaks in early/mid stages
- delusions (treat with antipsychotic)
  - particularly paranoid
  - beware 'delusions of theft' and 'misidentification delusions.' These may well be beliefs that have arisen as the artefact of cognitive impairment and/or to reflect neurological impairment (e.g. prosopagnosia) and are not likely to be antipsychotic responsive
- hallucinations
  - visual (up to 50% in LBD, although 20% of Alzheimer's patients will hallucinate at some stage during the course of the disease)
- sleep/wake cycle reversal/sundowning
- loss of insight/judgement
- wandering (60% of patients)
  - pacing and lapping (exclude akathisia)
  - (dangerous) eloping i.e. getting lost, accidents
- rejection of care
  - of food, hydration (consider artificial hydration) and hygiene

Complications

- eating and swallowing difficulties, cachexia
- infections – pneumonia, urinary tract
  - in pneumonias, the mortality is sevenfold that of a non-dementia patient
  - treat if symptomatic, antibiotics have limited efficacy
- falls – due to impulsivity, frailty, benzodiazepines and other sedatives
- pain – common in very elderly (50%)
  - may present behaviourally (non-verbally, crying, irritability)

- roughly 70% of patients with significant BPSD are likely to have under-treated or unrecognised pain as a contributing factor
- adverse reactions to drugs
  - antipsychotics – sensitivity (Lewy body disease), parkinsonism, akathisia, acute dystonic reactions, sedation, peripheral oedema, chest infections, accelerated cognitive decline, stroke risk (3 fold that of non-dementia patients, 1.5 fold mortality), hypotension
  - benzodiazepines – sedation, falls

Treatment

As curative treatment does not exist, ensure that end-of-life discussions/advance directives/appointment of enduring power of attorney all happen early before loss of capacity. The environment of care is important – it should be simple, safe, involve attentive and patient staff, include support and education for family and carers, person-centred, proactive, include distractions, activities, routine, memory cues and benign paternalism.

- Mild – cholinesterase inhibitors may have temporary cognitive benefit
- Moderate – focus on quality of life and maintenance of function
- Severe – maximise comfort, avoid aggressive, burdensome or futile treatments, avoid enteral tube nutrition, consider a secure facility, allow a natural death (AND)

Depression

In end-of-life care it is important to distinguish between clinical depression and profound sadness.

- depression is a pervasive sense of misery
- sadness is a normal response to loss which waxes and wanes but enjoyment and future planning are retained
- most terminally ill patients do not become clinically depressed
- prevalence is about 15% (compared with 5 to 10% in the general population), most commonly in the early cancer stages
- reaching a diagnosis of depression in terminal patients is difficult as the usual physical symptoms of depression in the otherwise well such as anorexia, weight loss, sleep disturbance are often already present in patients with malignant disease whether they are depressed or not
- the psychological symptoms are more discriminative
- asking 'Are you depressed?' provides a bed-side assessment of mood
- suicide is rare, however, fleeting suicidal thoughts and fluctuating 'will to live' in cancer patients are common and not necessarily pathological
- requests for euthanasia and/or physician assisted suicide are more common although, as for suicide, this is not limited to depressed patients
- clinical depression is under-recognised and under-treated yet it is generally very responsive to treatment
- the cause of depression is unknown but imbalances in neurotransmitters, especially serotonin, in the brain may play a part

Psychological symptoms of major depression may include

- hopelessness
- anhedonia (loss of pleasure)
- morbid guilt and shame
- worthlessness and low self esteem
- request for physician assisted euthanasia
- persisting suicidal ideation
- lowered pain threshold
- decreased attention and concentration
- cognitive slowing
- impaired memory
- indecisiveness
- early morning wakening
- ruminative negative thoughts
- nihilistic and depressive delusions
- feeling of unreality

Depression in older people and people with dementia

It is worth noting that the 'textbook' symptoms of major depression as they appear in references such as DSM-V have not been validated in older persons. Many older people with depression will not use the word 'depression' to describe their feeling state, but will instead use terms such as 'anxiety,' or 'I'm just worried, doctor.' Taking these terms at face value may lead to the inappropriate prescription of anxiolytics. Older persons also tend to express their depression more frequently in terms of somatic symptoms than younger persons do, which can clearly present diagnostic difficulties in a setting where palliative care is being provided.

Similarly, the diagnosis of depression in the setting of dementia is fraught. In cognitively intact populations, the diagnosis is made on the basis of symptom self-report. In advanced dementia, however, most patients will be unable to reliably verbalise their symptoms. The psychological distress that depression causes may instead be expressed in terms of externalising behaviours, which may include agitation, aggression, pacing and calling out, themselves common behavioural and psychological symptoms of dementia (BPSD). Two of the more reliable 'biological' symptoms of depression in the setting of dementia are recent worsening in sleep or appetite.

SSRI antidepressants are considered first-line pharmacological management for symptoms of BPSD. One of the likely reasons for their apparent success in controlling BPSD is that many cases labelled as BPSD are, in fact, cases of depression manifesting as disturbed behaviour. In a similar vein, while drug treatment trials of depression in the setting of dementia have been disappointing/contradictory, part of the problem inherent in such trials is a lack of certainty around diagnosis. In other words, these trials may well have included persons with undifferentiated BPSD, rather than depression.

A number of screening tools for depression in dementia exist. Perhaps the most commonly used tool is the Cornell Scale for Depression in Dementia. Clinicians should be wary of placing too much faith in the Cornell, however, as it has not been validated in patients with an MMSE of 10 or less, nor in patients with significant BPSD.

The role of antidepressants in treating depression in advanced dementia is controversial, and is likely to remain so, given the methodological problems in 'true case' ascertainment. When in doubt, however, clinicians are advised to err on the side of a trial of treatment.

Risk factors

- inadequate symptom control - unrelieved pain, nausea
- poor quality of life
- lack of social support
- past and/or family history of depression
- older age
- substance abuse
- misinformed prognosis
- polypharmacy
- specific drugs
  - steroids, cytotoxics, antibiotics, anti-hypertensives, neuroleptics, sedatives, beta-blockers, opioids
- immobility
- advanced malignant disease

Differential diagnosis

- adjustment/grief reaction (sadness)
- 'vital (physiological) exhaustion'
- demoralisation (a state of existential despair, meaninglessness and hopelessness but not of anhedonia and joylessness)
- delirium/sedation
- detachment (the terminal shedding of attachments)
- 'giving up' (affect neutral, rational, decisive)

Management

- mild to moderate depression
  - support, empathy, clarification of stressors or precipitators, explanation, cognitive therapy, symptomatic relief
- severe depression
  - supportive psychotherapy plus drug therapy
  - drug therapy - antidepressants are effective in 50 to 70% of cases
    - > a therapeutic trial is usually appropriate
    - > if in doubt, refer to a specialist psychiatrist
    - > SSRI e.g. escitalopram, sertraline, fluoxetine

        > although full response to antidepressant therapy may not be evident for 4-6 weeks, the lack of any response in the first 10-14 days should prompt consideration of a dosage increase or change of agent.
        > alternative agents include mirtazapine, duloxetine and venlafaxine
        > mirtazapine – can be useful due to its beneficial early effects on appetite, sleep and anxiety, which can be expected to occur well in advance of its antidepressant effects.
        > tricyclic antidepressants should be avoided, as the doses required for adequate response are likely to produce significant anticholinergic side effects, and may thus precipitate delirium, particularly in those with dementia.
    - psychostimulants e.g. methylphenidate
        > not as effective as SSRIs - may help retarded/withdrawn, frail patients for a few weeks only
        > a response may be achieved from small doses (5 to 30 mg each morning) within days either alone or in combination with an SSRI - watch for additive serotonergic effects. Modafinil may be a useful alternative to methylphenidate

Delirium

Toxic confusional states, like delirium, are common in people who are dying.

- if irreversible, may be an indication of impending death
- can be most distressing for patients, family and staff

Diagnosis

- abrupt onset, typically, but may be subacute in those with dementia.
- impairment of consciousness - the primary symptom which results in:
    - disorientation (to time)
    - fear and dysphoria
    - memory impairment (short term memory)
    - reduced attention span to external stimuli
    - hyperactive (frenzy) or hypoactive (retardation, torpor) but usually mixed hyperactive and hypoactive motor activity
    - reversal of sleep-wake cycle
    - perceptual disturbance (illusions, hallucinations)
    - disorganised thinking (paranoia, rambling)
    - dysgraphia (difficulties with writing)
- fluctuating symptoms ('sundowner effect')

Causes

There are often multiple organic causes but in up to 50% of cases, specific causes are not found, despite investigations. Diagnosis is dependent on the presence of an appropriate history, rather than the results of a 'delirium screen'. Causes may include:

- infection
- organ failure (liver, kidney) and underlying medical conditions

- drugs
  - sedatives
  - anticholinergics
  - opioids
  - benzodiazepine or alcohol withdrawal
  - steroids
- metabolic disturbances
  - dehydration
  - hypercalcaemia
  - hyponatraemia
  - hyper/hypoglycaemia
- hypoxia
- anaemia (severe)
- vitamin deficiency
- cerebral metastases
- cerebral haemorrhage
- epilepsy - post-ictal

Predisposing/precipitating/aggravating factors

- dementia and CNS immaturity
- any other cause of pre-existing cognitive impairment (e.g. intellectual disability, ABI)
- pain
- fatigue
- urinary retention
- constipation
- unfamiliar excessive stimuli
- change of environment
- sensory deprivation
- sleep deprivation

Management

- treat the underlying organic causes if identifiable and treatable
- treat fever, hypoxia, anaemia, dehydration, constipation, fear and anxiety and pain if possible
- ensure there is a safe and secure environment - have adequate staffing, remove potentially dangerous objects, have the mattress on the floor
- prevent sensory over-stimulation - have a single room, minimise noise and staff changes and maintain a warm and comfortable environment
- psychological interventions
  - reassurance
  - orienting aids (clock, personal belongings, presence of a supportive family member)

- cognitive strategies (clarification, reality testing, validation and repetition during lucid periods)
- emotional support (touch, empathy)

- drugs - use if symptoms are severe (in combination with above management)
  - antipsychotics (goal is to calm or pacify rather than sedate)
    - haloperidol is traditionally the drug of choice BUT not in AIDS delirium (HIV makes the CNS more sensitive to dopamine antagonists), hepatic encephalopathy or alcohol withdrawal where benzodiazepines only should be used (see haloperidol in drug section)
      - **Haloperidol regimen in acute delirium:**
      - Oral (tablets, liquid) if compliant, subcut if not
      - initial dosage - 0.5 to 1.5 mg orally
      - repeat and titrate every 30 to 40 minutes until controlled. In general, daily doses in excess of 3mg should be avoided due to high risks of extrapyramidal side effects (EPSE) in older patients. Only in physically robust, younger patients in whom significant aggression is present should doses in the order of 5-10mg daily be used.
      - maintenance - 50% of daily dose required to achieve control usually 1 to 3 mg/day (oral)
      - only add anticholinergic agent e.g. benztropine 1-2 mg if acute dystonia occurs. Routine use of anticholinergic agents will worsen delirium
      - extrapyramidal side effects are less pronounced with the parenteral route. Thus, if IV access is present, parenteral administration is preferable
    - risperidone (tablets, liquid, wafers) – dosage regimen as per haloperidol
    - olanzapine (tablets, wafers) – doses of up to 2.5mg TDS can be considered. Doses in excess of this tend to have significant anticholinergic activity, and may make things worse
    - Quetiapine – doses of 12.5-25mg are useful for acute sedation for short periods. Tolerance rapidly develops over several days to the sedative effects of this agent, leading to a tendency towards 'dose-creep' over time. If rapid control of distressing psychotic symptoms is required, however, this agent is not recommended, as it must be titrated up over several days in order to avoid both oversedation and postural hypotension.
  - sedatives (should not be used alone in most cases of delirium as they may aggravate symptoms, particularly if inadequate doses are used, so use with an antipsychotic)
    - benzodiazepines e.g. midazolam, clonazepam
    - barbiturates e.g. phenobarbitone
    - melatonin may be useful
  - anaesthetics e.g. propofol (rarely indicated)
  - drug-induced delirium
    - opioid-induced - decrease dose or change opioid
    - anticholinergic-induced - e.g. physostigmine may reverse this.

Even if the aetiology is irreversible, the symptoms of delirium may be palliated. Only 10 to 20% of patients with terminal delirium should require ongoing sedation to achieve control.

Disorders of sleep and wakefulness

Sleep disturbance in people who are dying is a frequent occurrence and it requires careful assessment and management.

- sleep patterns change with age and with illness e.g. cancer
  - reduction of depth and continuity of sleep and an increasing propensity for day-time naps occurs
  - many cancer patients have difficulty falling and staying asleep
  - cytokines are implicated in these changes

Insomnia

This is common and distressing. It undermines coping strategies through tiredness.

Causes

- poor symptom control of
  - anxiety, depression, pain, urinary frequency, faecal incontinence, nausea, vomiting, delirium, cough, delirium
- environmental changes
  - admission to hospital or hospice
  - disturbance by staff or family
- fear of going to sleep and never waking up
- drugs
  - stimulants e.g. methylphenidate
  - steroids (particularly if given after noon)
  - bronchodilators
  - alcohol, caffeine
- withdrawal of benzodiazepines, alcohol or tobacco

Management

- symptom control of above
- establish good sleep hygiene
  - regular bedtimes
  - minimise daytime napping
  - reduce evening stimulants e.g. caffeine, alcohol
  - comfortable bedding
  - comfortable temperature
- relaxation techniques
- drugs
  - hypnotics
    - > short acting benzodiazepines e.g. temazepam
    - > longer acting benzodiazepines e.g. oxazepam

    - > melatonin 2 to 4 mg at night
  - sedative antidepressants e.g. mirtazapine 7.5-15mg nocte
  - sedating antipsychotics e.g. quetiapine 25 to 50 mg at night may be considered if insomnia is resistant to above. Note that tolerance to sedation from quetiapine can occur rapidly (within several days).

Drowsiness/hypersomnia

These are common symptoms, particularly as the end-of-life approaches.

Causes

- organ failure e.g. renal, hepatic, cardiac, respiratory
- delirium (hypoactive)
- metabolic disturbances e.g. hyperglycaemia, hypercalcaemia
- fatigue or 'vital exhaustion'
- infection
- raised intracranial pressure
- drugs
  - adverse effects e.g. opioids, anticholinergics, benzodiazepines, cyclizine, levomepromazine (methotrimeprazine)

Management

- accurate assessment
- treat/remove causes where possible
- it may be unresolvable and be a natural part of the dying process

Sleep phase (circadian) disorder

(Delayed Sleep Phase Syndrome or Sleep-Wake Reversal)

- a dysregulation of the sleep-wake cycle
  - profound initial insomnia and
  - the inability to arise at desirable hours
- particularly associated with cerebral tumours
- presents a major burden for carers

Management

- shifting the circadian rhythm with behavioural strategies and bright light therapy is impractical in the terminally ill
- relief care for the family and a night nurse may be necessary as this tends to be an intractable symptom
- drugs are of limited benefit
  - sedatives e.g. benzodiazepines
  - psychostimulants e.g. methylphenidate can promote daytime alertness
  - sedating antipsychotics e.g. quetiapine 25 to 200 mg at night
  - pericyazine 20 to 30 mg at night
  - melatonin 2 to 6 mg at night

Terminal agitation

Perhaps best conceptualised as a prolonged delirium, this may indicate physical, psychological and/or spiritual discomfort. It is usually a 'pre-death' event.

A significant proportion of new-onset BPSD-type behaviours in fact represent terminal agitation. Early recognition of the syndrome enables appropriate palliative measures to be instituted early.

In the residential care setting, predictors of terminal agitation can include chest infections, unexplained fevers, poor oral intake, significant recent weight loss, the presence of bed sores, and increases in verbal and motor behaviours.

Terminal agitation is poorly recognised, and is often interpreted by care staff as a worsening of behavioural and psychological symptoms of dementia (BPSD). Early data from the Australian national Severe Behaviour Response Teams (SBRT) found that up to 10% of referrals to this service were ultimately revealed to have been on a terminal trajectory.

Causes

- physical discomfort
  - unrelieved pain
  - distended bladder or rectum
  - physical restraint
  - insomnia
  - uncomfortable bed or environment
- delirium (see delirium section)
- psychological discomfort
  - anger
  - fear
  - guilt
  - unfinished business
- spiritual discomfort/distress
  - helplessness
  - hopelessness
- drugs
  - akathisia induced by dopamine antagonists e.g. metoclopramide, haloperidol (and occasionally via sedating antihistamines such as promethazine)

Management

- assess and treat/remove possible causes
- explain what's happening to the family, patient (if appropriate) or main carers
- have the family present to reassure and support
- discuss psychological discomfort e.g. anger, fear, guilt
- drugs
  - see delirium section and anxiety and fear section

    - e.g. midazolam in inadequate doses can aggravate (by disinhibition) rather than relieve restlessness in some patients
    - if levomepromazine (methotrimeprazine) with a benzodiazepine are ineffective consider phenobarbitone or dexmedetomidine

Palliative sedation

This is considered when all other symptom-relieving measures have failed and the patient is clearly distressed.

Reasons for palliative sedation

- terminal restlessness (see terminal agitation)
- uncontrolled delirium (see delirium)
- severe breathlessness (see dyspnoea)
- massive haemorrhage (see haemorrhage)
- neurogenic or cardiogenic pulmonary oedema
- intractable distress

How palliative sedation is achieved

- the level of sedation should be titrated to removal of distress
- drugs
    - benzodiazepines e.g. midazolam, clonazepam
    - sedating antipsychotics e.g. levomepromazine (methotrimeprazine) (subcut 12.5 to 200 mg/24hours)
    - barbiturates e.g. phenobarbitone (subcut 600 to 1,200 mg/24 hours)
    - dexmedetomidine - experience in palliative care is limited
    - opioids
        - BUT increasing doses may not result in increased sedation (opioids tend only to be sedating in the opioid naive) and may instead induce respiratory depression or seizures

Sedation of this type may be subject to the principle of 'double effect' which has the dual effects of intentional relief of suffering and increased risk of hastening death. Palliative sedation itself has not been shown to hasten death.

Fear and anxiety

Fear

A brief, reflexive, rational and unpleasant emotional response (being afraid) caused by anticipation or awareness of danger. A present-focused, reality-based reaction initiating avoidant behaviours. Associated with physiological and psychological arousal. May be adaptive and enhance safety, or non-adaptive.

- innate fear (pain, bleeding, being alone, odours, confined spaces, novel places)
- learned fear (dying, death, being buried alive, needles, chemotherapy)

Anxiety

Sustained and excessive uneasiness. Future-focused, irrational, grossly exaggerated response to perceived threat to the 'self', to one's existence. An intrapsychic conflict. Encourages (unsuccessful) attempts to resolve threat.

- may be a normal alerting response
- may be a symptom of a medical condition (e.g. delirium, depression, hormone-secreting tumour), or a symptom of an impending medical catastrophe
- may be the result of an adverse reaction to a drug e.g. bronchodilators, steroids, methylphenidate
- may be a symptom of Generalised Anxiety, Panic or Depressive disorders

Common anxieties and fears centre on

- being ill
- separation from loved ones, homes or jobs
- becoming dependent on others (being a 'nuisance' or 'burden')
- losing control of physical faculties
- failing to complete life goals or obligations
- uncontrolled pain or other symptoms
- abandonment
- not knowing how death will occur
- 'death anxiety' (the fear of non-being)
- spirituality

Management of fear

- avoid threat if possible
- forewarning and preparations
- emotional first aid
- behaviour desensitisation for phobias (a syndrome of pathological fear)
- psychotropic medications of limited effectiveness

Management of anxiety

- careful listening and attention to detail
- support to maintain independence and autonomy
- honest and open discussion about the future with the patient and family at a pace that they can accommodate
- support realistic hope for the future
- provide distractions to avoid boredom and excessive self-reflection
- attend to social and financial problems
- provide focussed spiritual care if appropriate
- psychotropic drugs - may be a useful adjunct
  - benzodiazepines e.g. lorazepam can be very effective in the short term (days to weeks) but this may fade and there is a risk of tolerance and dependency
  - beta-blockers e.g. propranolol may block the peripheral symptoms and thus ease the unease

- antidepressants e.g. escitalopram, fluoxetine may be more effective longer term than benzodiazepines

Raised intracranial pressure

Raised intracranial pressure is a life-threatening event that needs to be carefully assessed and managed to optimise quality of life and minimise symptoms.

Symptoms

- severe headache which is worse when lying down or straining
- vomiting
- convulsions
- mental - drowsiness, delirium
- diplopia
- restlessness

Causes/risk factors

- cerebral metastases (more common with some primaries, e.g. lung, breast, melanoma than with others, e.g. prostate)
- primary brain tumour
- abscess
- cerebro-vascular event
- sagittal sinus thrombosis
- secondary hydrocephalus following surgery

Management

If raised intracranial pressure is suspected look for papilloedema and signs of cerebral irritation. Computerised tomography or MRI may be appropriate.

- raise the head of the bed
- consider cranial radiotherapy or neurosurgery for malignancy if prognosis/status warrants it
- drugs
  - dexamethasone up to 16 mg per day. Avoid doses after noon as may add to insomnia. Gradually reduce dose to minimum effective. Withdraw after 7 days if ineffective (note - some anticonvulsants can reduce effectiveness – see dexamethasone page)
  - codeine (sometimes eases head pain)
  - consider anticonvulsants particularly if seizures are present
  - consider acetazolamide 250 to 500 mg once daily to bd

Convulsions

Convulsions can be distressing not only for the patient but also for the family and other carers. They should be managed effectively to reduce distress and anxiety wherever possible. It is important to have a clear history of the convulsion in order to diagnose the type (grand mal, focal, absence or status epilepticus). At times a convulsion can be mistakenly diagnosed when the true cause of loss of consciousness or absence is a syncopal attack, cardiac arrhythmia, or a transient ischaemic attack.

Causes

- previously diagnosed epilepsy, brain trauma/surgery, brain tumour/mets
- drugs
  - some lower seizure threshold e.g. phenothiazines, tricyclics
  - interactions - antiepileptics have many variable and unpredictable interactions (see individual drug pages)
  - withdrawal e.g. of steroids, alcohol
- metabolic disturbance, e.g. hypoxia, hyponatraemia, hypoglycaemia

Management

Prophylaxis

- drugs
  - consider dexamethasone if related to raised intracranial pressure (primary brain tumour/metastases)
  - sodium valproate initially 500 mg bd to tds increasing every 3 days to 1 to 2 g per day
  - levetiracetam 500 mg bd initially
  - carbamazepine initially 100 to 200 mg once daily to bd increasing by 100 to 200 mg every 2 weeks to 800 to 1,200 mg per day – consider therapeutic drug monitoring of plasma concentrations
  - phenytoin 200 to 300 mg nocte - consider therapeutic drug monitoring of plasma concentrations
  - if oral route is not available consider
    - > clonazepam 1 to 4 mg/24 hours by subcut infusion
    - > midazolam 10 to 60 mg/24 hours by subcut infusion
    - > consider the use of phenobarbitone if convulsions are not effectively managed by other agents

Grand mal convulsions or status epilepticus management

- make the patient safe, explain what is happening and reassure
- drugs
  - rectal diazepam 10 to 20 mg
  - buccal midazolam 5 to 10 mg - between the cheek and gum
  - subcut boluses of clonazepam or midazolam
  - if these measures are not effective consider the use of phenobarbitone

Pain

The assessment and management of pain and other symptoms are the cornerstones of effective palliative care. There are different types of pain and many patients have more than one.

Comprehensive assessment

- listen to the patient's story and the language used
- ask about the site(s) of pain
- measure intensity with a validated tool to assess changes:
  - a visual analogue scale (some patients find this hard to use)
  - a numerical rating scale - perhaps the most common method used - patients rate their pain on a scale of 0 (no pain) to 10 (the worst pain they can imagine)
  - colour charts
  - facial expression charts
- ask about timing and duration of pain e.g. constant or episodic
- ask about the nature (e.g. stabbing, aching) and duration of the pain - this will determine management
  - identifies the type and source of pain
    - somatic nociceptive is usually constant and localised
    - visceral is usually described as deep or aching (capsular stretch pain) or intermittent and griping (colicky pain)
    - bone pain is usually deep or boring
    - neuropathic pain is usually burning, shooting or stabbing
- ask about what *relieves* the pain (body position, heat, cold) and what *exacerbates* the pain (movement, position, heat)
- ask about the significance of the pain
  - ask how much of a nuisance it is
  - discuss its significance
  - explain the likely causes - often helpful in allaying fears or anxieties and can significantly contribute to the relief of pain
- examine the part(s) that are painful - look, touch and move
- consider further investigation such as X-ray, CT or MRI but only if the result is going to influence management
- document all findings to compare and communicate
- review regularly - essential after any therapeutic intervention

Other assessment factors

In a bio-medical model of practice it is tempting to assume that pain has a predominant physical component. Often, physical pain is only part of the symptom complex (through direct or indirect tumour effects or non-malignant processes).

Psychological, spiritual and sociological elements will also be identifiable in many people with pain. Fear, anxiety, sadness, anger, frustration and isolation are but a few of the feelings that can contribute to the total perception of pain. All of these elements help to build a realistic picture of the overall impact of pain on the individual's quality of life.

Assessment in the setting of dementia

People living with dementia who require palliative care may not, by virtue of cognitive impairment, be able to validly report either the presence of pain, or the level of pain they are experiencing. There is good evidence that those with dementia are likely to be prescribed up to 50% less analgesia in acute hospital settings than those with comparable needs who lack a dementia diagnosis.

There are a number of validated pain assessment scales that can inform pain assessment in the presence of dementia. They include the Abbey Pain Scale, the PAIN-AD and the electronic ePAT (electronic Pain Assessment Tool), which uses facial coding to determine the presence of pain. These are screening tools only, and are no substitute for a comprehensive clinical assessment.

The emergence of new behavioural symptoms (such as withdrawal, agitation, anger, aggression and resistiveness to care) in a person with previously stable dementia symptoms should always be an indicator that pain may be an issue. It should be noted that the pain assessment tools mentioned above have not been validated in the presence of significant behavioural disturbance, as they do not reliably distinguish between pain and distress. In the absence of valid pain self-reporting in the setting of severe dementia, considering the views of a family caregiver who knows the patient and their usual behaviours well may be useful as part of the assessment process.

Unrecognised or undertreated pain can lead to the inappropriate prescription of psychotropic medication instead of adequate pain management.

Management

It is important to encourage patients to develop self-management strategies – recognising that this may not be possible in people with dementia – and to utilise non-pharmacological strategies such as rest, positioning, pacing etc. There are also a number of enabling strategies like goal setting, pain management plans, scripts and diaries that many will find useful.

Analgeics

- some pains may not respond completely to opioids
- co-analgesics are useful when response to opioids is poor
- switching route can sometimes help e.g. from oral to subcutaneous

- in prescribing analgesics use a step-wise approach:

		morphine or oxycodone or hydromorphone* or fentanyl or methadone
	codeine or dihydrocodeine or tramadol or buprenorphine	
	regular paracetamol	
paracetamol or NSAIDs e.g. diclofenac, naproxen		
co-analgesics, specific therapies e.g. radiotherapyy		

- regular paracetamol may be useful in opioid induced hyperalgesia although use should be continued only if effective as up to 8 tablets per day adds significantly to the tablet burden
- there is some debate over the second step in this ladder
  - most palliative care practitioners go to step 3 either after step 1 or initially depending on the severity of the pain
  - pain relief from codeine may be from the active metabolite, morphine
  - the place of tramadol in palliative care remains unclear - it can be extremely emetogenic

Initiating morphine in opioid naive patients

- start with small regular oral (if possible) immediate release doses
- titration with slow release morphine is less common than with immediate release
- if using immediate release prescribe morphine elixir (immediate release) (2.5 to 5 mg) every four hours regularly and titrate
- prescribe 'when required' doses of ⅕th to ⅙th of the regular 24 hour dose for 'breakthrough', 'episodic' or 'incident' pain
- document the amount of morphine taken
- once a stable dosing regimen is achieved (2 to 3 days) convert to a long-acting preparation
  - calculate the total 24 hour dose of immediate release morphine required from 'breakthrough' and regular dosing, divide by 2 and give twice daily
  - 'when required' doses of ⅕th to ⅙th of the regular 24 hour dose should be prescribed as immediate release once again for pain between doses
- if the patient can no longer swallow
  - give ½ the total 24 hour oral dose by continuous subcutaneous infusion
  - 'when required' doses of ⅕th to ⅙th of the regular 24 hour dose should be prescribed once again for pain between doses

*** Drugs that are either not available or not funded in New Zealand**

- consider reducing dose if another mode of pain relief is used (e.g. radiotherapy, ketamine)

Initiating oxycodone in opioid naive patients

- start with small regular oral (if possible) doses
- prescribe oxycodone immediate release capsules or liquid every 4 to 6 hours and titrate
- prescribe 'when required' doses of $^1/_{10}$th to $^1/_{12}$th initially (although many practitioners use $^1/_5$th to $^1/_6$th) of the regular 24 hour dose for 'breakthrough', 'episodic' or 'incident' pain
- document the amount of oxycodone taken
- once a stable dosing regimen is achieved (2 to 3 days) convert to a long-acting preparation
  - calculate the total daily dose of oxycodone required from 'breakthrough' and regular dosing, divide by 2 and give twice daily
  - 'when required' doses of $^1/_{10}$th to $^1/_{12}$th initially (although many practitioners use $^1/_5$th to $^1/_6$th) of the regular 24 hour dose should be prescribed as immediate release for pain between doses
- consider reducing dose if another mode of pain relief is used (e.g. radiotherapy, ketamine)
- the long acting preparation has a layer of immediate acting drug round it
- if the patient can no longer swallow
  - give ½ the total 24 hour oral dose by continuous subcutaneous infusion
  - 'when required' doses of $^1/_{10}$th to $^1/_{12}$th initially (although many practitioners use $^1/_5$th to $^1/_6$th) of the regular 24 hour dose should be prescribed once again for pain between doses
- consider reducing dose if another mode of pain relief is used (e.g. radiotherapy, ketamine)

Initiating hydromorphone in opioid naive patients*

- as with oxycodone start with small regular oral (if possible) doses
- titrate upwards in small increments as with morphine and oxycodone
- otherwise the same principles apply

Initiating fentanyl patches in opioid naive patients

- don't - fentanyl patches should only be used in patients who have already been exposed to opioids

Initiating methadone in opioid naive patients

- as methadone has a long and variable half life it should be commenced at low dosage e.g. 1 mg to 2.5 mg bd and consideration should be given to dose reduction once at steady state (minimum 5 days)
- should be used under advice of a specialist palliative care physician only

*** Drugs that are either not available or not funded in New Zealand**

Adverse effects of opioids

- all opioids are associated with the following adverse effects but the incidence (incidences below are for morphine) and severity vary from opioid to opioid (e.g. fentanyl is less constipating than morphine)
- tolerance to some of these adverse effects can develop e.g. nausea/vomiting but not to others e.g. constipation
  - constipation - 95% of patients (less with fentanyl [50%] and the naloxone/oxycodone combination product) - prescribe a laxative prophylactically
  - nausea/vomiting - 30-50% of patients - usually in the first 10 days until tolerance develops
  - drowsiness - 20% of patients - usually in the first 3 to 5 days until tolerance develops
  - confusion - 2% of patients - either reduce the dose, change to a different opioid or consider adding haloperidol. Rates of worsening confusion are greatly elevated in those with a pre-existing cognitive impairment, due to diminished cognitive reserve. Frank delirium can be precipitated.
  - hallucinations/nightmares - 1% of patients - give haloperidol or change to a different opioid
  - hyperalgesia - usually to touch as a result of too high a dose of opioid which may improve on dose reduction
  - hyperkatafeia - emotional lability induced by long-term opioid use

Opioid rotation

- opioid rotation (or changing from one opioid to another) is often used when tolerance to the analgesic effects of opioids (stimulation of NMDA receptors) or severe adverse effects occur
- works because of the difference in the mix of opioid receptors stimulated by each individual opioid in each patient
- most often from morphine to oxycodone, fentanyl or methadone
- rotation should only occur under supervision and by a specialist as conversion doses are difficult to predict and are often much smaller doses than those listed below - see oxycodone, hydromorphone*, fentanyl and methadone in the second section

Opioid equivalents

- the following are 'single dose' equivalences i.e. ONLY equivalents in healthy volunteers given a single dose
- equivalence in sick patients who are chronically dosed is difficult to quantify - use care when converting from one opioid to another

*** Drugs that are either not available or not funded in New Zealand**

- pethidine is NOT recommended in palliative care

codeine	60 mg oral	=	6 mg oral morphine
tramadol	100 mg oral	=	10 mg oral morphine
oxycodone	5 mg oral	=	10 mg oral morphine
	5 mg subcut	=	5 mg subcut morphine
hydromorphone*	6 mg oral	=	30 mg oral morphine
	2 mg subcut	=	10 mg subcut morphine
methadonesee	methadone page in the 'Drug information' section		
fentanyl	see fentanyl page in the 'Drug information' section		
buprenorphine	see buprenorphine page in the 'Drug information' section		

Co-analgesics

- drugs usually used for a different indication with analgesic properties (sometimes such use is outside the product license)
- can be used in combination with other analgesics or alone
- choice is determined by the types of pain
- the use of co-analgesics is probably most helpful in neuropathic pain
- bone pain - due to tumour or metastatic involvement
  - NSAIDs e.g. diclofenac - inhibit prostaglandins
  - bisphosphonates e.g. pamidronate, zoledronic acid
  - denosumab*
- skeletal muscle spasm pain - due to tumour involvement
  - muscle relaxants e.g. diazepam, clonazepam, baclofen
- smooth (intestinal) muscle spasm pain - 'colic' from intestinal spasm
  - anticholinergic/antimuscurinic e.g. hyoscine butylbromide
- tenesmus - due to tumour or metastatic involvement of the rectal muscles
  - steroids e.g. dexamethasone, prednisone - decrease inflammation around tumour
- raised intracranial pressure - due to tumour or fluid
  - steroids e.g. dexamethasone - decrease inflammation around tumour
  - NSAIDs e.g. diclofenac - inhibit prostaglandins
- liver capsule stretch pain - from an enlarged liver
  - steroids e.g. dexamethasone - decrease inflammation

Neuropathic pain

- often the most severe and difficult to manage of all persisting pains
- caused by damage to the nervous system
- involves NMDA receptor stimulation to some extent
- severity cannot usually be linked to the amount of damage
  - 'trivial' lesions can produce severe pain

*** Drugs that are either not available or not funded in New Zealand**

Causes

- peripheral nerve damage - post-surgical, post-trauma or compression
- herpetic nerve invasion
- amputation - phantom limb pain
- Chronic Regional Pain Syndrome (CRPS)
- nerve root injury - traumatic avulsion, post-spinal surgery
- epidural scarring, arachnoiditis
- spinal cord injury and disease
- stroke
- diabetes
- chemotherapy e.g. vincristine, oxaliplatin, taxanes, cisplatin

Characterisation

- characterised by description and by cause
  - BUT the pain is not always within the distribution of a dermatome or a peripheral nerve
- includes allodynia (pain in an area of altered sensitivity) and other sensory symptoms
- generally continual and of varying intensity
  - variability in intensity is spontaneous and often has a paroxysmal component not necessarily related to stimulation
- descriptive terms include burning, cutting, stabbing sharp/shooting crushing
- episodic pain, which can be present on top of the continuous pain, may itself be brief but often a long-lasting aching pain remains for several hours

Management

- a multidisciplinary approach is useful
- behavioural modification - any treatment will be of only limited value unless certain behaviours are changed so address cognitive, mood and behavioural aspects of the patient's pain individually or in a group
- drugs
  - opioid analgesics (first line for neuropathic pain) should be trialed but doses may increase rapidly - some opioids may be more useful than others e.g. methadone which has NMDA blocking activity
  - centrally acting agents reduce spinal hyperexcitability
  - some drugs have an effect on nociceptor neuromodulators, neurotransmitters and cell membrane stability
  - efficacy is highly variable between drugs so tailor the drug to the patient
    - > gabapentin, pregabalin*
    - > anticonvulsants e.g. valproate
    - > benzodiazepines e.g. clonazepam
    - > tricyclic antidepressants e.g. nortriptyline SSRIs e.g. escitalopram, sertraline - limited efficacy in palliative care

*** Drugs that are either not available or not funded in New Zealand**

  > SNRIs e.g. duloxetine*, venlafaxine
  > antiarrhythmics e.g. mexiletine
  > muscle relaxants e.g. baclofen
  > NMDA antagonists e.g. ketamine
  > alpha-adrenergic agents e.g. clonidine
  > calcium channel blockers e.g. nifedipine
  > steroids e.g. dexamethasone for nerve pressure pain
  > sodium channel blockers e.g. lignocaine*
- combining an antidepressant with an anticonvulsant or similar may be more effective than either alone e.g. nortriptyline + gabapentin, pregabalin* if the above are ineffective consider intrathecal/epidural opioids, local anaesthetics and clonidine

• other analgesic modalities
  - nerve blocks
    > availability is dependent on the skills of the team
    > access to a specialist anaesthetist is not always possible
    > for pain which breaks through analgesia, or is controlled at rest but not on movement or is nonresponsive
    > upper abdominal pain due to pancreatic cancers may respond to coeliac plexus blocks
  - others - often used in conjunction with analgesics
    > mobilisation e.g. structured stretching, progressive resistance training
    > radiotherapy/surgery
    > cytotoxic drugs
    > hormone therapy
    > spinal delivery systems
    > neuromodulation e.g. transcutaneous nerve stimulation (TENS) and, very occasionally, implanted devices such as peripheral nerve or spinal cord stimulation

*** Drugs that are either not available or not funded in New Zealand**

Gastrointestinal system

Nausea/vomiting

These are common symptoms in palliative care and are often difficult to control.

- it is important to separate nausea from vomiting
- consider how each affects the individual patient
  - a vomit a day with no nausea may be more acceptable than continuous low-level nausea
  - for some patients, nausea is more distressing than pain
- nausea and/or vomiting often has more than one cause
- choose a management strategy to fit the cause(s)
- antiemetics work at differing sites and receptors
- antiemetics that affect multiple receptors in multiple areas, such as levomepromazine (methotrimeprazine), may be useful choices regardless of cause
- a combination of antiemetics is useful, particularly where there are multiple causes

Causes

There are two distinct areas in the central nervous system (CNS), which are predominantly involved with nausea and vomiting:

- chemoreceptor trigger zone (CTZ) close to the area postrema
  - part of the central nervous system, the CTZ is thought to lie outside the blood/brain barrier and so can be affected by causes and treatment which are unable to penetrate the CNS
- the vomiting centre in the medulla oblongata
  - can be directly stimulated or inhibited by certain agents

The CTZ sends impulses to the vomiting centre, which then initiates nausea and/or vomiting. Higher centres involved with fear and anxiety also communicate with the vomiting centre, as do the peripheral vagal and sympathetic afferents and the vestibular nerve.

The causes can be summarised as:

- higher centre stimulation - fear/anxiety
- direct vomiting centre stimulation - radiotherapy to the head, raised intracranial pressure
- vagal and sympathetic afferent stimulation - cough, bronchial secretions, hepatomegaly, gastric stasis, constipation, intestinal obstruction
- chemoreceptor trigger zone stimulation - uraemia, hypercalcaemia, drugs e.g. opioids, cytotoxics
- vestibular nerve stimulation - motion

Management

- higher centre stimulation (emotion - fear/anxiety)
  - counselling/explanation/listening
  - a benzodiazepine

- direct vomiting centre stimulation (radiotherapy to the head, raised intracranial pressure)
  - cyclizine
  - dexamethasone
- vagal and sympathetic afferent stimulation (cough, bronchial secretions, hepatomegaly, gastric stasis, constipation, intestinal obstruction)
  - cough - see 'Cough' p. 45
  - bronchial secretions - see 'Excessive (retained) secretions' p. 47
  - constipation - see 'Constipation' p. 35
  - hepatomegaly
    - dexamethasone
    - cyclizine
  - gastric stasis
    - domperidone (minimal extrapyramidal effects)
    - metoclopramide
    - erythromycin - a strong prokinetic
  - intestinal obstruction
    - cyclizine
    - levomepromazine (methotrimeprazine)
    - avoid prokinetics e.g. metoclopramide in complete obstruction although use in partial obstruction may help - see 'Intestinal obstruction' p. 38
- chemoreceptor trigger zone stimulation (uraemia, hypercalcaemia, drugs e.g. morphine)
  - haloperidol
  - levomepromazine (methotrimeprazine)
- vestibular nerve stimulation (motion)
  - cyclizine
  - hyoscine patch (scopolamine)
- other drugs which may be useful where others have failed
  - atypical antipsychotics e.g. olanzapine
  - ondansetron, palonosetron* (may cause constipation) - experience in palliative care is limited
  - aprepitant (a neurokinin 1 (NK1) antagonist from the class of drugs known as substance P antagonists) - used with steroids and ondansetron for delayed emesis following highly emetogenic chemotherapy. Its place in palliative care has not been established.
- other therapies with little evidence include acupuncture, ginger, cannabis

*** Drugs that are either not available or not funded in New Zealand**

Bowel management

- alteration in bowel function is common in terminally ill people
- constipation is more common than diarrhoea
- efficient bowel management may alleviate distress
- carefully assess bowel function on a daily basis
- regimens should be discussed, carried out and reported on daily

Constipation

- diagnose through an accurate history followed by examination
- it is the difficult or painful and infrequent passage of hard stools
- comparison with an individual's normal bowel habit and usual use of laxatives may highlight changes related to disease or treatment
- a record of bowel habits will help in the management
- examination of the abdomen and the rectum may exclude faecal impaction or rectal pathology

Causes

- metabolic disturbances e.g. hypercalcaemia
- dehydration from vomiting, polyuria, sweating, tachypnoea
- drugs
  - cytotoxics e.g. vinca alkaloids (via neuropathies)
  - opioids via opioid receptors in the GI tract and perhaps in the CNS - > 95% of people taking morphine will become constipated although other opioids may be less constipating e.g. fentanyl, methadone
  - anti-cholinergics e.g. tricyclic antidepressants
  - aluminium salts in antacids
  - iron
  - antispasmodics e.g. hyoscine butylbromide
  - anti-Parkinsonian drugs e.g. levodopa
  - antipsychotics/anxiolytics
  - ondansetron, palonosetron*
- immobility e.g. weakness
- low fibre diet e.g. milky/invalid foods or reduced intake
- inability to obey the call to stool
- concurrent medical problems e.g. haemorrhoids, anal fissure, diabetes, hypothyroidism
- intestinal obstruction from tumour, faeces or adhesions (abdominal X-ray may help with diagnosis)
- gastrointestinal tract nerve compression or damage or autonomic neuropathy

Symptoms

- anorexia
- vomiting/nausea

*** Drugs that are either not available or not funded in New Zealand**

- abdominal discomfort or cramping
- spurious diarrhoea or overflow
- confusion
- anxiety
- bowel obstruction
- pain

Management

- prevention is the key
- if a cause (or causes) are identified remove it (or them) if possible
- exercise reduces the risk of constipation so encourage it where possible
- encourage increased fibre e.g. bran, kiwi crush or soluble fibre formulations (require activity and fluids to avoid impaction)
- laxatives
  - when opioids are prescribed anticipate constipation and prescribe an oral softener with a stimulant laxative e.g. docusate with senna or bisacodyl which may prevent the need for rectal intervention later (NB if combinations cause cramps reduce the dose or use an osmotic laxative such as macrogol 3350 with electrolytes (Movicol™, Lax-Sachets™)
  - low dose opioid antagonists such as naloxone (marketed in combination with oxycodone and methylnaltrexone*) are effective in opioid-induced constipation without affecting analgesia
  - if constipation is already present give a bisacodyl 10 mg suppository and a glycerin suppository or a sodium lauryl sulphoacetate enema (Micolette™)
  - avoid stimulant laxatives in people with signs of GI obstruction
  - if the patient has a partial obstruction use an osmotic/softener laxative e.g. docusate, and avoid stimulant laxatives
  - if the patient has a spinal cord compression where evacuation is difficult keep the bowel motion firm (avoid softeners) and use a stimulant
  - if a patient taking laxatives has no bowel motion for two days and this is not their normal bowel habit give extra laxatives and, if appropriate, kiwi fruit or prune juice
  - if a patient taking laxatives has no bowel motion for three days and this is not their normal bowel habit a rectal examination should be carried out
    - > if soft faeces are found give 2 bisacodyl 10 mg suppositories or 1 to 2 Micolette™ enemas
    - > if hard faeces are found give 1 or 2 glycerine suppositories or 2 bisacodyl 10 mg suppositories or consider macrogol 3350 with electrolytes (Movicol™, Lax-Sachets™)
    - > if rectum is empty (or no result from first action) repeat abdominal palpation and consider an abdominal X-ray
  - suppositories must make contact with the bowel wall to work
  - methylnaltrexone*

*** Drugs that are either not available or not funded in New Zealand**

- faeces consist of approximately 50% water, 25% bacteria and 25% food residue so even if the patient is not eating there will be faeces in the bowel

Diarrhoea

- a relatively uncommon problem in palliative care
- rotation from morphine to fentanyl may result in a sudden reduction in opioid constipating effects resulting in diarrhoea

Causes

- faecal impaction (overflow) - identify with a clinical examination (including rectal)
- colo-rectal carcinoma (also causes discharge and tenesmus)
- loss of sphincter tone and sensation e.g. from spinal cord compression
- incomplete gastrointestinal obstruction - frequent or recurrent diarrhoea suggests partial obstruction so try lower bowel evacuation
- malabsorption or food intolerance e.g. from lack of pancreatic enzymes
- concurrent disease e.g. diabetes mellitus, hyperthyroidism, inflammatory bowel disease
- radiotherapy to the torso
- cytotoxics (e.g. capecitabine)
- antibiotics - *C.difficile*
- bowel surgery or inflammation
- anxiety
- opioid rotation to a less constipating opioid e.g. from morphine to fentanyl

Management - dependent on cause

- assess bowel habit and faecal consistency
- consider likelihood of infection
- maintain skin integrity around anal area - use barrier creams to prevent excoriation e.g. zinc oxide
- think about overflow from impaction or partial obstruction
- use abdominal examination or X-ray to rule out obstruction
- restrict oral intake (except fluids) to rest the bowel
- withhold laxatives where appropriate
- administer antidiarrhoeal medications such as loperamide, opioids
- if impacted use manual removal followed by laxatives
- in partial obstruction, diarrhoea may be very unpleasant
- in spinal cord compression, a constipating drug may help e.g. codeine, loperamide (although patients already receiving morphine may not benefit) followed by regular suppositories and/or manual removal
- in colo-rectal carcinoma a palliative colostomy or radiotherapy should be considered
- in malabsorption states, the addition of pancreatic enzymes at meal times will help the situation e.g. pancreatin or, in bile salt malabsorption, cholestyramine
- secretory diarrhoea (associated with carcinoid syndrome or AIDS) may respond to octreotide

- ondansetron or palonosetron* may be worth considering especially if nausea/ vomiting are also present

Intestinal obstruction

Intestinal obstruction is a difficult area of palliative care. There is considerable inter-individual and intra-individual variation in symptoms and optimal management.

Causes

- can be mechanical or paralytic
- blockage of intestine by intraluminal or extraluminal tumour, inflammation or metastasis
- blockage can occur at multiple sites in patients with peritoneal involvement
- may be aggravated by drugs e.g. anticholinergics, opioids
- radiation fibrosis
- autonomic nerve disruption by tumour

Management

The management of intestinal obstruction should be tailored to the individual at the time with different strategies being employed when needed.

- explain the predicament
- give dietary advice e.g. foods with minimal residue
- minimise colic by stopping osmotic/stimulant laxatives (continue softeners) and give subcutaneous hyoscine butylbromide (20 mg bolus followed by 60 to 80 mg subcut infusion over 24 hours)
- give analgesia (commonly subcutaneous opioids)
- reduce vomiting by giving appropriate antiemetics e.g. cyclizine with or without haloperidol - metoclopramide should only be used if there is clear evidence that there is only a partial obstruction
- consider alternative measures e.g. surgery, radiotherapy
- steroids e.g. dexamethasone should be given a trial
- iv fluids and nasogastric tubes should be avoided but may be preferred where drug treatment has not worked. Subcut fluids may have a role in some
- somatostatin analogues (octreotide) may be used subcutaneously in specialist practice to reduce secretions and minimise symptoms
- if subacute intestinal obstruction, the aim may be to clear the obstruction using steroids e.g. dexamethasone to reduce the inflammation around the obstruction and hyoscine butylbromide to minimise secretions and colic then, at an appropriate time, to push gut contents through with a prokinetic agent e.g. metoclopramide
- the timings of each change in therapy will depend on the individual patient and their condition
- review the situation regularly

*** Drugs that are either not available or not funded in New Zealand**

Mouth care

Poor oral hygiene is probably the most significant factor in the development of oral disease near the end-of-life.

- good mouth care is essential to the wellbeing of patients debilitated by advanced disease
- mouth problems are common - occurring in up to 90% of patients
- risk factors for oral problems include
  - debility, dry mouth (drugs, mouth breathing, radiotherapy), chemotherapy, dehydration, cachexia, weight loss, ill-fitting dentures

Assessment/causes

- appropriate and effective oral assessment should be carried out on each patient daily using a pen torch and spatula
- remember functions of saliva – cleansing and lubrication, buffering, remineralisation, antimicrobial, digestion, maintenance of mucosal integrity
- key questions for effective mouth care are
- is the mouth dirty, dry, painful or infected?
- also assess mental, nutritional and physical state, concurrent medications, tongue, teeth/dentures, mucous membranes, type of saliva, and lips
  - mental state will determine the patient's ability and willingness to participate in their care
  - nutritional state will give an indication of the patient's ability to chew and swallow as well as their general wellbeing - a well balanced diet and adequate fluid intake are important in mouth care
  - physical state may also contribute to mouthcare issues e.g. low haemoglobin increases susceptibility to infections and may be accompanied by lethargy, weakness and dyspnoea, all of which contribute to mouth care problems
  - patients in pain may require extra help with their mouth care
  - concurrent medications can affect the state of the mouth e.g. opioids/ antidepressants may cause dry mouth, steroids/antibiotics may encourage oral candidiasis
  - other causes of poor mouth care include debility, reduced oral intake, inability to brush teeth, dehydration, saliva-reducing drugs, chemotherapy or radiotherapy, oxygen therapy and mouth breathing

Management - prevention is a priority

- regular tooth and denture brushing, twice daily at least
- regular use of anti-bacterial and anti-fungal mouthwash
- consider using oral probiotic lozenges
- check fit of dentures
- regular dental checks if possible
- regular mouthcare; frequency dictated by assessment
- check for infection
- check for bone or nerve damage
- check mucosa

- reduce caffeine and alcohol, diet drinks (have a low pH)
- hypersalivation may be helped with atropine eye drops 1%, 1 to 2 drops in the mouth 3 to 4 times a day, ipratropium bromide nasal spray, 1 to 2 puffs in the mouth 3 to 4 times a day, radiotherapy or botulinum toxin to salivary glands

Dirty mouths

- chlorhexidine mouthwash is a useful cleansing agent
- sodium bicarbonate mouthwash is used by many, especially in oncology
- there is little point in cleaning the mouth if dentures are worn unless those dentures are also meticulously cleaned (including soaking overnight in ¼ strength Milton™)

Dry mouths

- salivary stimulants e.g. lime juice, fresh melon or pineapple are useful in dry mouths as is a saliva substitute (often useful to freeze fruit first); also, lollies or mints (sorbitol, xylitol-containing gum)
- pilocarpine solution (1 mg/mL, 5 to 10 mL or 1 to 2 drops 4% eye drops rinsed three times a day) may be useful for dry mouths

Infected mouths

- nystatin suspension is useful in the treatment of oral candidiasis but may take up to two weeks to clear an infection and many candidal infections are now resistant to it
- miconazole oral gel is also useful in the treatment of oral candidiasis, usually after nystatin suspension has failed
- systemic anti-fungals e.g. fluconazole (50 mg a day for 7 to 14 days or 100-150 mg stat) are sometimes needed for intractable oral candidal infections
- aciclovir may be useful for herpetic infections

Painful mouths

- may need systemic opioids
- coating agents
  - sucralfate suspension (use crushed tablets)
  - topical anaesthesia e.g. lignocaine viscous (watch for choking hazards)
- benzydamine is an analgesic mouthwash for painful mouths
- topical corticosteroids e.g. triamcinolone in orabase may be useful for aphthous ulcers (not used if oral candidiasis present)
- Bonjela™ (choline salicyclate) may soothe sore gums

Taste alteration

- reduction in taste sensitivity i.e. hypogeusia
- absence of taste sensation i.e. ageusia
- distortion of taste i.e. dysgeusia

Causes

- local disease of mouth and tongue
- systemic diseases
- partial glossectomy
- nerve damage
- zinc deficiency
- alteration to cell renewal via malnutrition, metabolic endocrine factors, viral infections, hyposalivation
- dental pathology/hygiene
- diabetes
- gastric reflux
- drugs
  - cyclizine
  - anticholinergics (leads to dry mouths)
  - chemotherapy
  - lithium
  - ACE inhibitors
  - citalopram (uncommon)

Management

- remove or treat causes e.g. give, pilocarpine for dry mouth, stop likely drugs
- zinc (but only if zinc is deficient)
- use sialogogues such as chewing sugar-free gum or sour-tasting drops
- may be unresponsive to interventions

Swallowing difficulties

Swallowing oral formulations of drugs often becomes difficult for palliative care patients.

- drugs which are available in the capsule form may be more easily swallowed using the 'leaning forward' technique
  - this involves bending the head down rather than tipping it back when swallowing capsules
  - when leaning the head down and forward the capsule floats to the back of the throat ready to be swallowed
  - the standard way of swallowing solid oral formulations - head is tipped back- results in the capsule floating to the front of the mouth making swallowing the capsule difficult
  - this 'leaning forward' technique will not work for tablets as they do not float so use the standard tilting the head back approach
- if swallowing remains an issue consider crushing tablets or opening capsules if appropriate (do not crush slow or modified release or enteric coated solid dose forms), oral liquids or other routes e.g. subcut, intranasal, sublingual, rectal

Malignant ascites

This is a common symptom in patients with breast, colon, endometrial, ovarian, pancreatic or gastric cancers.

Assessment

- consecutive measurements of abdominal girth
- respiratory function - shortness of breath may occur
- early fullness e.g. squashed stomach
- portable ultrasound examination

Causes

- peritoneal fluid build-up in the abdomen due to a failure of the lymph system to adequately drain
- tumour in the peritoneal cavity
- low serum albumin
- excess fluid production
- venous compression or vena cava/hepatic vein thrombosis

Management

Symptoms usually appear at > 1L of fluid in the abdomen.

- if the prognosis is short and the symptoms are not troublesome then no action may be needed
- explanation of the problem and likely outcomes may be enough to allay fears or anxieties
- if the symptoms warrant further intervention, the bowel is not distended or the ascites is not loculated, consider paracentesis
- beware of loculation - use of ultrasound is now common
- suction may be used if the fluid is viscous, e.g. of ovarian origin
- drain no more than 2L in the first hour then drain slowly for 12 to 24 hours (to a maximum of 5L in 24 hours)
- place an ostomy bag on the site once the paracentesis needle is removed to collect any residual leaking fluid
- check biochemistry frequently
- some centres advise daily measurement of girth
- a surgical opinion, for the insertion of a peritoneo-venous shunt, may help in recurrent ascites if the patient's life expectancy is greater than 3 months

repeated drainage may be followed by rapid reaccumulation

- drugs
  - if the patient is fit for diuretics, give spironolactone 100 mg (or more) with or without frusemide 40 mg once daily although benefit is often extremely limited
  - for gastric stasis give a prokinetic e.g. metoclopramide
  - if there is evidence of liver capsule stretch pain use a steroid e.g. dexamethasone - see 'Co-analgesics protocol' p. 30

Respiratory system

Respiratory symptoms are among the most common at the end-of-life. Dyspnoea (breathlessness), for example, can occur in more than half of patients who are dying, and the incidence increases as death approaches. In addition, cough, haemoptysis, hiccup and pleural pain are present in a considerable number of people who are dying.

Dyspnoea (breathlessness)

Breathlessness is one of the most common and distressing symptoms for both patients and relatives as the end-of-life approaches.

- it has a reported incidence of 29 to 74% of people near the end-of-life
- the distress caused by breathlessness should not be underestimated
- a careful evaluation of the nature of the breathlessness is important
- listening to the descriptors (the language that the patient uses to describe the sensation) of the quality and quantity of breathlessness is important in choosing management
- breathlessness will only rarely be expressed in purely physical terms
- the assessment of breathlessness should use a multidimensional approach, as with the assessment of pain
- identifying the cause(s) is an essential step in effective management

Causes

- it is often multifactorial
- it is not always possible to identify one treatable cause
- impaired performance (can be broken down further into a number of separate entities)
  - airflow obstruction
    - this can be related to large airways (tumour producing either extrinsic or intrinsic obstruction, laryngeal palsy, radiation stricture)
    - or smaller airways (asthma, emphysema, chronic bronchitis, lymphangitis carcinomatosis)
  - decreased effective lung volume (effusions, ascites, pneumothorax, tumour, lung collapse, infection)
  - increased lung stiffness (pulmonary oedema, lymphangitis carcinomatosis, pulmonary fibrosis, mesothelioma)
  - decreased gas exchange (as above plus pulmonary emboli, thrombotic tumour, tumour effect on pulmonary circulation)
  - pain (pleurisy, chest wall infiltration, rib/vertebral fractures)
  - neuromuscular failure (paraplegia, motor neurone disease, phrenic nerve palsy, cachexia, paraneoplastic syndromes)
  - left ventricular failure (congestive heart failure)
  - ascites/pleural effusion
- increased ventilatory demand (due to anxiety, anaemia, metabolic acidosis)

Assessment

- careful assessment of each situation to identify probable causes is an essential starting point
- pay particular attention to the descriptions the patient gives of the sensation and experience of breathlessness and ask specifically, 'How would you describe your breathlessness today?'
- severity and meaning for each individual is important as dyspnoea may have a variable effect on quality of life at the end-of-life, varying with the cause(s) and the individual's perception of the meaning of the symptom
- in a broad sense, dyspnoea has at least five main components, each of which must be attended to
  - sensation (what it feels like)
  - perception (how it is viewed in the context of the illness)
  - distress (does it cause suffering or grief?)
  - response (how individuals react)
  - reporting (the language used to relay these elements)

Management

- treat/remove causes where possible with treatments that are similar to those used in general medicine
  - the cancer itself together with radiation or chemotherapy
  - the complications of cancer e.g. pleural effusions, anaemia
  - concurrent non-cancer causes e.g. heart or lung disease
- non-pharmacological management
  - psychosocial support
    - address anxiety and fear by active listening and exploration of the meaning of breathlessness
    - explanation and reassurance
    - relaxation techniques
    - relearning breathing patterns and control
    - discuss coping strategies
  - positioning
  - adaptation and energy conservation which is often most effectively undertaken with the help of occupational or physiotherapists or specialist nurses
  - physiotherapy
  - drainage of effusions or ascites
  - blood transfusion may be useful if anaemia is present and it is appropriate
  - bronchial stents, brachytherapy
  - complementary therapies e.g. aromatherapy
  - music engagement, therapy and the arts
  - draughts of fresh air using fans and open windows
- at the end-of-life non-pharmacological interventions become less effective so greater reliance on drugs is common, although both may be used together

- drugs
  - opioids (usually morphine as efficacy of others have not been studied)
    - > oral/parenteral - oral seems to be more effective than subcutaneous
    - > doses are usually small 2.5 to 10 mg prn
  - oxygen
    - > a draught of fresh air may be as effective as oxygen so only use in hypoxic patients
    - > efficacy of oxygen varies between patients but if saturations are < 90% oxygen may have some benefits
  - nebulised normal saline
  - bronchodilators (nebulised/inhaled) e.g. salbutamol
    - > for patients with reversible airway obstruction
  - corticosteroids e.g. dexamethasone
    - > for patients with lymphangitis carcinomatosis, bronchial obstruction or radiation pneumonitis
  - benzodiazepines (short acting) e.g. midazolam
    - > in anxious or fearful patients where other methods have failed
  - antibiotics e.g. amoxicillin
    - > if infection is suspected may decrease secretions
  - diuretics
    - > if congestive heart failure or pulmonary oedema are present
  - anticholinergics e.g. hyoscine, glycopyrrolate
    - > if secretions are bothersome - see excessive (retained) secretions

Cough

Cough is often associated with other symptoms such as dyspnoea, wheezing or chest tightness. It is a defensive mechanism - like pain - and it can have a detrimental effect on the quality of life as it interferes with communication, food and drink intake and sleep.

Causes and treatment

- acute respiratory infection
  - antibiotic (if appropriate), physiotherapy, nebulised saline
- airways disease
  - bronchodilator e.g. salbutamol, inhaled or systemic corticosteroids, physiotherapy
- malignant obstruction (tumour)
  - as above but consider nebulised local anaesthetic
- oesophageal reflux
  - prokinetic agents e.g. metoclopramide, positioning, proton pump inhibitors e.g. pantoprazole
- salivary aspiration
  - anticholinergic agent e.g. hyoscine

- cardiovascular causes
  - usual cardiac drugs
- pulmonary oedema
- drugs which can cause cough
  - angiotensin converting enzyme inhibitors e.g. captopril - change or discontinue therapy

Management

- cough with tenacious sputum i.e. a productive cough
  - may respond to steam inhalation, nebulised saline, bronchodilators or physiotherapy
- drugs (as above and below)
  - cough suppressants e.g. codeine, pholcodine, morphine
    - may be useful in dry non-productive coughs
    - titrate dose to effect
    - may not be appropriate in productive coughs as retaining the mucus may encourage infection
  - Simple linctus
    - this is a soothing syrup which may be an effective first choice
  - paroxetine (for itch of the respiratory tract)
  - nebulised local anaesthetics e.g. lignocaine (lidocaine)
    - may be useful in intractable cough
    - patients should not eat or drink for at least an hour after using the nebuliser to avoid accidental inhalation of food or drink
    - potential to cause bronchospasm so the initial dose should always be given under medical supervision
  - oxygen
    - may be useful in cough associated with emphysema
  - corticosteroids e.g. dexamethasone, prednisone
    - often used to treat cough associated with endobronchial tumours, lymphangitis or radiation pneumonitis

Hiccup

This is a respiratory reflex characterised by spasm of the diaphragm resulting in a sudden inspiration and closure of the vocal cords. Hiccup is a most distressing symptom and should be attended to with urgency. The phrenic and vagal nerve and the brain stem are involved.

Causes

- gastric distension
- diaphragmatic irritation
- phrenic or vagal nerve irritation
- uraemia

- neurological disease affecting the medulla e.g. brain stem tumour, infarction, encephalitis
- liver disease (hepatomegaly)

Management

- remove any correctable cause
  - e.g. reduction in gastric distension with a prokinetic - metoclopramide - if not obstructed
- pharyngeal stimulation with cold water
- elevation of pCO2 using paper bag rebreathing or breath holding
- phrenic nerve block may be considered
- drugs
  - corticosteroids e.g. dexamethasone, prednisone
  - antipsychotics e.g. haloperidol, chlorpromazine, levomepromazine (methotrimeprazine)
  - muscle relaxants e.g. baclofen
  - benztropine
  - anticonvulsants may be useful if a CNS cause is present e.g. phenytoin, valproate, carbamazepine
  - gabapentin

Several of the above may have to be tried. None are consistently reliable.

Excessive (retained) secretions

This phenomenon occurs when a patient is too weak to clear respiratory secretions particularly near the end-of life.

- air passing through these secretions produces a gurgling or rattling sound ('death rattle') which, although not obviously distressing to the patient may be distressing for families and carers
- reassurance that the patient is not distressed is important for families

Causes

- inability to swallow or clear secretions
  - salivary or bronchial secretions
- cessation of steroids in patients with cerebral involvement can lead to neurogenic pulmonary oedema which may not respond to the management below - consider continuation of steroids in these patients

Management

- appropriate positioning to allow postural drainage
- drugs
  - anticholinergics e.g. hyoscine butylbromide, hyoscine hydrobromide, glycopyrrolate
    - > can help but are often started too late in life to effect a major change as secretions already present have to evaporate first

    - hyoscine hydrobromide may cause delirium while glycopyrrolate and hyoscine butylbromide do not get into the CNS readily
- occasionally suction is needed to remove plugs of mucus but is not always successful and should be avoided if possible

Haemoptysis

The coughing up of blood from the lungs, or haemoptysis, is often a frightening symptom for both patient and family.

Causes

It is not always possible to identify the cause and it has been suggested that up to 40% of cases remain undiagnosed.

- tumour erosion - lung or oesophagus
- infection
- pulmonary embolism
- clotting disorders

Management

- treat/remove the causes if appropriate
- if minor coughing up of blood i.e. flecks or spots of blood
  - not usually helpful to give any specific treatment but patient reassurance may help
- if the bleeding is persistent or is major
  - haemostatics such as tranexamic acid may be useful (1 to 1.5 g, 2 to 4 times daily)
  - consider radiotherapy which may have some benefit
- if the bleeding is massive
  - the normal 'life saving' interventions of bronchoscopy and intubation are inappropriate
  - reduce the patient's awareness, fear and anxiety with subcutaneous midazolam (2.5 to 10 mg) with or without subcutaneous morphine
  - staff should stay with the patient and family until the immediate crisis is over

Skin

Itch (pruritus)

Itching can be as unpleasant and disruptive as pain and can have just as adverse an effect on quality of life.

- nerve fibres involved in the itch process are anatomically very similar to those involved in pain with opioid receptors being involved in both pathways
- cholestatic and uraemic itch in particular are mediated via opioid receptors
- the skin can be affected by many metabolic, pharmacological, dietary, environmental and psychological factors
- an accurate history of the onset and nature of itching is essential and will help to identify a cause along with examination of the skin for signs of disease
- not all itch is histamine related
- serotonin and prostaglandins may also be involved
- both central (neuropathic) and peripheral (cutaneous) itch have been identified

Causes

- hepatic/renal disease (obstructive jaundice, cholestatic and uraemic itch)
- drug allergy
- drugs e.g. opioids, vasodilators
- endocrine disease
- iron deficiency
- lymphoma
- provocative sensory influences such as rough clothing
- parasites

Management

- treat/remove causes
- attempt to break the itch/scratch cycle by short clipping nails, wearing cotton gloves, applying paste bandages
- apply surface cooling agents with emollients e.g. 0.25 to 1% menthol in aqueous cream, tepid showers, humid environment
- avoid washing with soap and use emulsifying ointment instead and Alpha-keri™ as bath oil
- light therapy may help
- drugs
  - oral anti-histamines e.g. promethazine, cetirizine
  - bile sequestrant e.g. cholestyramine 4 to 8 g per day
  - night sedation e.g. temazepam
  - H2 antagonists (act on histamine receptors in the skin) e.g. cimetidine 400 mg twice daily
  - NSAIDs e.g. diclofenac
  - anxiolytics e.g. benzodiazepines

- chlorpromazine 10 to 50mg TDS
- steroids e.g. dexamethasone (lymphoma itch), topical hydrocortisone
- rifampicin 150 to 300 mg per day (chronic cholestasis)
- 5HT3 antagonists e.g. ondansetron (uraemic)
- gabapentin (uraemic)
- doxepin capsules or cream
- thalidomide
- paroxetine, mirtazapine (paraneoplastic itch)

Referral to a specialist dermatologist should be considered at an early stage if no alleviation of symptoms is obtained.

Sweating

Sweating is an unpleasant and debilitating symptom that affects not only the patient but often indirectly, the carers as well. As with many other symptoms it can indicate physical, psychological and/or environmental disturbance.

Causes

- environmental temperature changes
- emotion
    - usually confined to the axillae, palms and soles
- lymphomas, hepatic metastases and carcinoid
    - may produce drenching night sweats
- intense pain precipitating or manifesting through anxiety and fear
- infection
- drugs
    - alcohol
    - antidepressants (especially venlafaxine)
    - opioids

Management

- treat/remove causes
- drugs
    - NSAIDs e.g. diclofenac
        - act via prostaglandins in the hypothalamus
    - cimetidine 400mg to 800 mg at night
        - acts on histamine receptors in skin
    - steroids e.g. dexamethasone
    - paracetamol (for night sweats)
    - gabapentin
    - glycopyrrolate topically

Pressure injury care

Pressure injuries occur when the blood supply is shut down by pressure e.g. from a hard bed or other surface resulting in tissue death.

Causes

- pressure on one particular part of the body
  - sitting is riskier than lying as more of a person's weight can press on a smaller area e.g. buttocks while sitting
- sliding patients against a surface can cause damage to skin (friction) or tissue (shear)
- wetness increases the risk of pressure injury damage

Assessment

- A comprehensive assessment should include:
  - clinical history
  - pressure injury risk scale
  - skin assessment
  - mobility and activity assessment
  - nutritional assessment
  - continence assessment
  - cognitive assessment
  - assessment of extrinsic risk factors

Management

- avoid causes
- assess using appropriate 'risk factor scale' at regular intervals i.e. daily for high risk, weekly for low risk
- use pressure relieving aids and mattresses when these are available and assessed as being needed
- use aids to movement where appropriate
- discuss management with patient and home carers
- use a semipermeable adhesive dressing if at risk
- where semipermeable adhesive dressing is not practical use meticulous hygiene followed by povidone iodine spray
- higher rating pressure injuries should be treated as wounds with appropriate dressing products and techniques
- rubbing over pressure injuries should be discouraged
- turn bed-fast patients every 2 to 4 hours as appropriate
- in incontinent patients protect vulnerable skin with zinc and castor oil cream and consider catheterisation
- if nutritional state is poor, get dietary advice from a dietitian
- inform primary carers of management on discharge from in-patient facility

Lymphoedema

As lymphoedema (swelling of a limb [usually] due to fluid) cannot be cured, the aim of treatment is to achieve maximal improvement and long-term control.

Causes

- damage to the lymphatic drainage system allows fluid to build up
- the protein in the initial oedema draws more fluid out of the blood
- the protein in the fluid also encourages inflammation
- infection may occur

Management

- provide analgesia if painful
- early referral to an appropriately trained professional (usually a physiotherapist) produces best results
- success requires the patient's full cooperation, so management may be suboptimal in those with significant cognitive impairment. In others, a simple explanation of lymph flow and the cause of swelling is essential, together with instruction on daily skin care
- infections must be cleared before commencing treatment
- gentle massage of the affected area helps to shift fluid from one area to another, local practitioners in the techniques may be available
- regular measurement of both normal and affected limbs is essential to monitor progress
- in most cases containment hosiery of an appropriate size and strength should be worn all day, complemented by specific exercises and massage if possible
- if the limb is not in a suitable shape or condition to use hosiery or if the fingers are swollen, compression bandaging or taping may be necessary for approximately 2 weeks
- diuretics are not usually useful (except when the patient has heart failure or hypoalbuminaemia), may be detrimental and can cause dehydration

Fungating wounds and tumours

Fungation of wounds or tumours (smelly, exuding necrotising wounds) presents an obvious manifestation of disease that can cause major distress to patient, carers and family.

- 'fungating' wounds are malignant in nature and combine ulceration with proliferation
- usually seen in the area of the breast or head and neck
- as healing of the wound is rare, the aim in managing these wounds is to achieve maximum patient comfort together with a reduction in the distortion of body image
- odour is often caused by anaerobic bacterial infection of compromised tissue
- the wound may bleed as blood vessels are eroded

Causes

- primary skin tumour e.g. melanoma, squamous cell carcinoma

- invasion of nearby tissue by underlying tumour e.g. breast cancer
- metastatic involvement

Management

- ensuring that the area is as clean as possible can help to reduce smell and exudate
- many preparations are recommended for odour reduction and each practitioner will have their favourite e.g. lemon oil
- as the odour is often due to anaerobic infection, metronidazole gel applied directly to the wound can be helpful
- for excessive exudate wound dressings may be used on the advice of a local expert - disposable nappies may be an option
- bismuth idoform paraffin paste (BIPP) may help in drying up the wound and reducing odour
- many fungating wounds are painful - use systemic analgesics
- morphine injection added to a gel in a clean environment and used topically may help (0.05 to 0.1% morphine [i.e. 0.5 to 1 mg/mL] in Intrasite™ gel, metronidazole gel or KY Jelly™)
- radiotherapy, chemotherapy and hormone manipulation should be considered for some tumours
- if bleeding consider pressure with adrenaline 1:1000 soaked swabs

Systemic effects of terminal diseases

Paraneoplastic syndromes

The remote effects of cancer can be classified as paraneoplastic syndromes. They are thought to be rare, affecting perhaps only 1% of people with cancer. These syndromes may be identified before the diagnosis of cancer is made.

Dermatological syndromes

There are a number of skin disorders that herald the presence of underlying malignant disease. Consultation with a specialist dermatologist is advised.

- acanthosis nigricans (treatment generally ineffective)
- dermatomyositis (treatment requires removal of the cause but symptoms may be managed with corticosteroids)
  - associated with lung, breast, ovarian, pancreatic, stomach, colorectal cancers and non-Hodgkin's lymphoma
- acquired ichthyosis (treat the underlying cause)
- paraneoplastic pemphigus (use steroids and ciclosporin)

Metabolic syndromes

- hypercalcaemia - see 'Hypercalcaemia section' p. 60
- Cushing's syndrome (ectopic secretion of ACTH)
- SIADH - syndrome of inappropriate antidiuretic hormone secretion
  - results in hyponatraemia which is common near the end-of-life
  - symptoms appear at plasma sodium concentrations <125 mmol/L and include stupor, coma and seizures

Neurological/psychiatric syndromes

- Lambert-Eaton myasthenic syndrome (LEMS)
  - associated with small-cell lung cancer
  - manifests as muscle weakness and fatigue
  - may respond to immunosuppression, plasmapheresis and 3,4 diaminopyridine (3,4 DAP)
- sub-acute cerebellar degeneration
  - associated with ovarian and lung cancer
- polymyositis
  - associated with non-Hodgkin lymphoma, lung cancers, bladder cancers
- motor neuropathy
  - associated with lymphoma
- peripheral neuropathy
  - associated with small-cell lung cancer
- limbic encephalitis
  - changes in mood, personality

- memory impairment (recent more than remote)
- seizures

Management

All of these syndromes are usually irreversible and treatment is largely symptomatic.

Venous thromboembolism

Venous thromboembolism (VTE) includes both deep vein thrombosis (DVT) and pulmonary embolism (PE). It is a lethal disorder that is common in people with cancer and to a lesser extent in other advanced diseases.

Diagnosis/symptoms

- PE - episodic and otherwise unexplained breathlessness or confusion tachypnoea, and pleuritic chest pain - may be difficult to interpret in the presence of other pulmonary pathology
- DVT - pain or tenderness and swelling, increased warmth, oedema and redness
- tests such as D-Dimers are generally unhelpful in advanced cancer but Doppler scans may reveal DVTs in large veins.

Causes and risk factors

- malignant disease
- recent chemotherapy or surgery
- immobility
- malignant pelvic disease
- familial (hereditary factors)
- age (over 40)
- obesity

Management

If the patient is at risk of VTE

- take into account any risk of bleeding and expected prognosis
- discuss with the patient and family (an important proxy for those with advanced dementia) whether they want to have active prophylaxis with anti-embolism stockings and low molecular weight (LMW) heparin as appropriate, balancing risks and benefits to optimise quality of life
- if the patient is in the last few days or weeks of life then thromboprophylaxis is often not appropriate, and is not routine - the best evidence in favour of thromboprophylaxis is in potentially reversible co-existing acute conditions

Treatment for VTE (DVT- includes prevention of PE and/or recurrent thrombosis)

- anticoagulation with a LMW heparin e.g. enoxaparin should be started immediately unless there is a contraindication - the preferred option because it is more effective in VTE associated with malignancy, and if dosed properly is less likely to cause bleeding

- LMW heparin followed by warfarin or dabigatran is cheaper and perhaps more convenient, but warfarin requires blood tests (INR may be very difficult to keep stable in those with advanced disease and variable nutritional intake)
- re-assess the patient regularly to confirm the management plan is appropriate to the stage of their illness and their wishes
- if warfarin is used start at the same time as LMW heparin and continue the LMW heparin for 2 days after achieving therapeutic INR
- haemorrhagic complications occur in almost 50% of people with advanced cancer (due to drug interactions or hepatic dysfunction)

Weakness/fatigue

Weakness and fatigue are amongst the most common and debilitating symptoms at or near the end-of-life.

- it is often assumed that weakness is an inevitable consequence of approaching death BUT there are many factors that may exacerbate or precipitate weakness
- careful assessment may result in interventions that can improve quality of life
- there are often two main contributing factors
  - cachexia
    - a debilitating state of involuntary weight loss complicating chronic malignant, infectious and inflammatory diseases that contributes to mortality
  - asthenia
    - fatigue or lassitude
      - easily tired and a decreased capacity to maintain adequate performance
    - generalised weakness
      - anticipatory subjective sensation of difficulty in initiating a certain activity

Causes

Cancer related

- cachexia (see cachexia section)
- decreased food intake
  - nausea, vomiting, constipation, intestinal obstruction, diarrhoea, malabsorption, 'squashed stomach syndrome' in hepatomegaly, tumours, ascites, mouth and throat problems including infection, poor teeth, thrush, taste alteration
- metabolic problems
  - hyponatraemia, uraemia, liver failure, hypercalcaemia, anaemia from any cause
- emotional causes
  - anxiety, depression, fear, isolation, apathy, stress
- neuromuscular damage by tumour
  - to brain, spinal cord, peripheral nerves

- paraneoplastic syndromes e.g. Lambert Eaton myasthenic syndrome, motor neuropathy
- radiotherapy and chemotherapy
- insomnia
- depression

Non-cancer related

- drugs
  - long-term steroids
  - some psychotropics
  - diuretics
  - antihypertensives
  - oral hypoglycaemics
  - statins
- neurovascular problems
  - transient ischaemic attacks, motor neurone disease, myasthenia gravis, Parkinson's disease, peripheral neuropathies
- metabolic diseases
  - diabetes mellitus, Addison's, hyper/hypothyroidism, tuberculosis, subacute bacterial endocarditis, connective tissue disorders

Management

- establish and, where possible, treat or remove cause
  - review the drug regimen
  - correct metabolic abnormalities
- give dietary advice/support
  - increase calorific intake if possible and appropriate
- exercise
  - exercise may be effective particularly in fatigue caused by radiotherapy
  - limited exercise programmes have been shown to be beneficial even in those close to the end-of-life
- drug therapy
  - hormones e.g. megestrol acetate, medroxyprogesterone
    - mechanism of action is unclear but dose related weight gain, improved calorie intake and improved sense of well-being have been reported
    - effect on fatigue is thought to be minimal
  - prokinetic antiemetics e.g. metoclopramide
    - decrease nausea and vomiting, increase food intake and appetite
    - no evidence of weight gain has been reported
  - steroids e.g. dexamethasone
    - weight gain and fat deposition has been documented but with no increase in lean body mass
    - benefit may be transient

- eicosapentaenoic acid (EPA) and nutritional support in combination with anti-inflammatory agents (COX2 inhibitors) have been used
- stimulants e.g. methylphenidate, modafinil

Although these drugs may be effective in some patients with fatigue potential benefit should be weighed against adverse effects e.g. long-term steroids causing muscle weakness.

Cachexia

Cachexia can be distressing for both the patient and their family and carers. It is difficult to watch a person 'waste away' and is often perceived as a sign of impending death.

- cachexia is derived from the Greek kakos (bad) and hexis (condition)
- defined as a multifactorial syndrome with ongoing loss of skeletal muscle mass that cannot be fully reversed leading to progressive functional impairment
- diagnosis - weight loss greater than 5%, or 2% in individuals already showing depletion
- develops progressively through various stages - precachexia, cachexia, and refractory cachexia
- refractory cachexia or cancer anorexia cachexia syndrome - very advanced cancer (preterminal), active catabolism low performance status (WHO score 3 or 4), and life expectancy less than 3 months
- may complicate many chronic or end-stage diseases in addition to cancer
- not starvation, which can be reversed with nutrition
- distinct from age-related loss of muscle mass, primary depression, malabsorption syndromes and hyperthyroidism
- in the setting of advanced dementia, the presence of cachexia will often reflect a deteriorating oral intake over the preceding weeks/month rather than a more traditional 'ominous' cause. Declining oral intake leading to significant weight loss is a poor prognositic sign in this group, however, and its presence may be a marker that the person with dementia is entering a palliative stage of management

Causes

The metabolic mechanism of the progressive wasting is uncertain.

- complex metabolic and catabolic processes occur with cytokines playing a major role
- tumour initiates an inflammatory response probably mediated by tumour-derived proinflammatory cytokines (interleukin-1, interleukin-6, interferon-gamma, tumour necrosis factor-alpha)
- cancer cachexia involves inflammation, hypermetabolism, neuro-hormonal changes, and the proteolytic and lipolytic factors
- enhanced substrate cycling (fat, carbohydrate and protein) occurs which is associated with metabolic inefficiency, weight loss and a suboptimal response to nutritional support ('anabolic blockade')
- neural pathways controlling energy homeostasis are disturbed (particularly the hypothalamic melanocortin system), promoting catabolic activity

Assessment

Cachexia should be considered if the patient has lost ≥ 5% of their body weight and/or has a BMI < 20 kg/m2 and 3 out of the following are present

- decreased muscle strength
- fatigue or reduced physical activity
- anorexia
- low fat-free mass index (low muscle mass)
- abnormal biochemistry
  - CRP > 5 mg/L
  - IL-6 > 4 pg/ml
  - Hb < 12 g/dL
  - serum albumin < 32 g/L

Treatments

- favourite foods
- un-pressured eating
- referral to a dietician
- drugs (efficacy is minimal for most)
  - dexamethasone 4 mg/day for 5 days
  - medroxyprogesterone
  - megestrol
  - EPA (up to 2 g per day)
  - cannabinoids
  - prokinetics e.g. metoclopramide
  - antidepressants e.g. mirtazapine
  - thalidomide
  - olanzapine

Anaemia

A significant proportion of people with advanced or chronic disease are anaemic. symptomatic anaemia usually presents when the haemoglobin is below 80 g/L although, if chronic, patients may adapt to this concentration

Symptoms

- fatigue
- delirium
- dyspnoea
- dizziness (postural hypotension)
- exacerbations of angina/heart failure

Causes (often multiple)

- chronic disease (normocytic)
- haemorrhage (microcytic, low iron levels)

- bone marrow failure (pancytopenic)
- malnutrition (macrocytic, folate and iron deficiencies)
- chronic renal failure (reduced erythropoietin production)

Management

- blood transfusion
  - rarely improves symptoms significantly for any length of time BUT may be considered, prior to further active treatment or a significant family event
  - it is often easier to give a transfusion rather than deal with the negotiation involved in not treating although the latter may be more appropriate
  - time, attention to detail and information for the patient and the family are all essential in the decision making and consent process
- erythropoietin
  - expensive, not readily available and response can be slow and limited

Hypercalcaemia of malignant disease

The symptoms and signs of hypercalcaemia are often insidious in their onset. It can be classified as a paraneoplastic syndrome.

- should be considered in patients who have vague symptoms
- consider appropriateness of treatment BEFORE a calcium concentration
- if the patient has a serum calcium > 2.6 mmol/L consider treatment

Symptoms

- thirst and dehydration
- increased urinary output
- constipation
- loss of appetite
- nausea and or vomiting
- fatigue
- pain - usually back and abdominal
- confusion, depression

Causes

- bone metastases
- increased bone metabolism
- decreased renal clearance of calcium
- dehydration
- enhanced absorption from the gut

Management

- make the diagnosis
- decide about the most appropriate course of action together with the patient, family and team
- consider stopping diuretics, vitamin D and calcium

- the aim is to provide symptom relief and reduce serum calcium to an acceptable level using minimal intervention
  - mild to moderate (serum calcium 2.6 to 3 mmol/L)
    - > initially oral then, if necessary, iv rehydration
    - > consider steroids
  - moderate to severe (serum calcium 3 to 3.5 mmol/L)
    - > initially iv or subcut rehydration
      - ~ 2 to 3 L normal saline/24 hours
    - > then iv/subcut bisphosphonate (may take 72 hours to work)
      - ~ pamidronate 90mg iv infusion (can be given as a subcutaneous infusion)
      - ~ zoledronic acid 4mg iv infusion can be used but is significantly more expensive
      - ~ calcitonin may be useful when bisphosphonates begin to fail

Nutrition in palliative care

Good nutritional advice from a dietician improves patients' quality of life.

- ensuring food choices that are
  - of good quality and attractively presented
  - appealing on multiple sensory levels (sight, taste, aroma, texture) to maximise cues to eating, particularly in those with impaired cognition
  - appropriate to the patients' cognitive level (e.g. provision of finger foods where the ability to use cutlery has been lost)
  - appropriate to the maintenance of quality of life

    not detrimental to the patient i.e. aggravate nausea, or be of a difficult texture/ moisture content to swallow
  - preferred foods which may entail lifting dietary restrictions and discussing with the patient's family that food intake is no longer for the purpose of sustaining life and fuelling bodily processes
- providing an environment that allows for social interaction around meal times i.e. central dining room, playing of music during meal times
- note that for people with advanced dementia, a quieter environment that minimises distractions during mealtimes may be more useful.
- maintaining comfort
- providing weight gain may be appropriate initially but during the terminal phase it is not an appropriate nutrition intervention goal

In some instances, it may become inappropriate to hydrate or feed a patient, these cases should be discussed by a multidisciplinary team on a case by case basis.

A dietitian can provide

- complete nutrition assessments
- nutritional care plans considering an individual's life expectancy, treatment plan and overall functional status
- assessments of nutritional factors impairing the patient's physical and psychological wellbeing

- patient-centred strategies such as food fortification, meal timing/frequency and oral nutrition support
- flexible menus by liaising with catering staff to enable inpatients to enjoy their preferred foods
- an advocate role for the patient (both for and against) regarding more aggressive forms of nutrition support on a case by case basis
- clarification for the team and the patient the place of artificial nutrition when the patient is approaching the terminal phase

Organ failure

Renal failure

The following does not apply to patients who are being dialysed. For information on drug dosing during dialysis consult a renal specialist or drug information service.

Symptoms

- oedema (from sodium and water retention)
- restless legs (may respond to clonazepam, very low dose gabapentin)
- itch (from raised urea or phosphate)
- nausea/vomiting (from increased toxins)
- fatigue (from anaemia)

Management

- the same as those outlined in the relevant sections e.g. nausea/vomiting
- when pain is an issue remember that
  - morphine's metabolite is renally cleared so use fentanyl or methadone instead (or perhaps oxycodone)
  - NSAIDs increase sodium and water retention, are nephrotoxic and if urea is raised risk of GI bleed increases so avoid

Drug dosing

- as the kidneys fail creatinine plasma concentrations will rise
- many labs now report an estimated glomerular filtration rate (eGFR) - there is some debate as to whether this can be used to adjust the doses of renally cleared drugs
- to calculate how well the kidneys are functioning, calculate creatinine clearance in mLs/minute using the Cockcroft and Gault equation:

Creatinine clearance (CrCl)

$$\text{CrCl (mLs/min)} = \frac{\text{(140-age) x ideal body weight (kg)}}{\text{plasma creatinine (umol/L) x 0.8}} \quad \text{(x 0.85 if female)}$$

(ideal body weight = 50kg + 0.9kg for each cm above 150cm (replace 50kg with 45 kg if female)

- the creatinine clearance is important in the dosing of renally cleared drugs e.g. gabapentin or drugs whose metabolites are renally cleared e.g. morphine (see end section)

- for drugs that are almost completely renally cleared the dose regimen is a proportion of the normal dose:

$$\text{Adjusted dose} = \frac{\text{calculated creatinine clearance}}{100\text{mL/min}} \times \frac{\text{normal dose}}{1}$$

Hepatic failure

End stage liver failure is usually seen with liver metastases, liver primary and/or past alcohol abuse/hepatitis.

Symptoms

- raised liver enzymes
- jaundice
- ascites
- itch
- encephalopathy
- low albumin and raised INR

Drug dosing

- there is no single marker for liver dysfunction but albumin concentrations and INR are a measure of how well the liver can clear drugs (its metabolic capacity)
- doses of metabolised drugs (drugs that are mainly cleared from the body by the liver rather than the kidneys i.e. approx 70% of drugs) should be adjusted in severe liver failure (albumin of < 30 g/L and an INR of > 1.2) by approximately 50% especially drugs with low therapeutic index e.g. antidepressants, antipsychotics, opioids, paracetamol, anticonvulsants, NSAIDs

Management is the same as that outlined in the relevant sections.

Cardiac failure

The treatment of patients with end stage cardiac failure centres around the relief of the accompanying symptoms:

- dyspnoea
- cough
- fatigue
- immobility
- oedema

Treatment of the symptoms is the same as for other causes in palliative care.

Perhaps the most difficult part of the management of these patients is when and how to discontinue the many cardiac medications prescribed (See Deprescribing section following). As yet there is no clear evidence for the order or rate of discontinuation. Negotiation with patient, family and cardiologist may produce agreement on a process for this. Once swallowing becomes a problem consideration should be given to stopping medications.

Deprescribing in palliative care

Deprescribing is the process of ceasing inappropriate medications safely and effectively.

- an individualised process, focusing on the patient, and taking into account their physical function, comorbidities, preferences, and lifestyle
- an ongoing process as medicines that were initially appropriately prescribed may become inappropriate over time
- often not carried out in palliative care when it perhaps should be e.g. in cancer patients who are transitioning from curative to palliative treatment or in terminally ill patients on medications with long term benefits only e.g. statins
- important because polypharmacy may lead to an underuse of essential medications and a reluctance to start new medications and an increased risk of harm due to the 'prescribing cascade', where more medications are prescribed to treat the side effects of others
- always consider the time required to obtain the expected benefits from medications vs expected life expectancy

Benefits

- improved quality of life
- reduced pill burden
- reduced potential adverse drug reactions
- improved medication adherence

Triggers

- older patients presenting with falls, delirium, or cognitive impairment
- development of adverse drug reactions
- worsening physiological function (cardiac/hepatic/renal failure)
- transition of care moments (hospital <=> home <=> palliative care unit <=> nursing home/respite)
- end-of-life

Enablers for deprescribing

- fear of increased adverse effects, addiction or tolerance.
- inconvenience of medication taking

Barriers to deprescribing

- patient reluctance
- feelings of hopelessness (e.g. 'not worth treating anymore').
- family pressure to continue treatment, and concern from general practitioners about stopping medications first prescribed by medical specialists.

When deprescribing a medication remember that the pharmacodynamics and pharmacokinetics of other medications may be affected; use recognised tools as a starting point -

- Beers criteria
- STOPP (Screening Tool of Older Person's Prescriptions)
- START (Screening Tool to Alert doctors to Right Treatment)
- anticholinergic risk scale

The deprescribing process

- take a comprehensive medication history
- ascertain indications, compliance, and potential adverse reactions
- use medication review/reconciliation services provided by pharmacists if available
- estimate life expectancy and identify any medications unlikely to provide meaningful benefit
- set goals and create a plan e.g.
  - reduced pill burden to the patient, adverse drug reactions
  - improved symptom relief and the quality of life
- emphasise that if medications are being ceased, it is not because the patient is not worth treating, but rather that the medications are causing harm or have no benefit
- relax targets of therapy e.g. levels for blood pressure, blood sugar levels, and whether blood tests should be performed
- deprescribe one or two medications at a time, not all at once
- consider a trial withdrawal to determine continuing efficacy
- provide education around what to do if symptoms return or withdrawal reactions occur
- a multidisciplinary approach should be used, with all involved and informed in the process

Common deprescribing

- anti-hypertensives
  - monitor blood pressure post cessation, as many patients remain normotensive
  - beta-blockers need to be weaned slowly to prevent rebound hypertension/ tachycardia. NB use caution when ceasing in heart failure
- aspirin - time to benefit usually exceeds life expectancy
- diuretics - do not deprescribe if being used for symptomatic treatment or for heart failure
- statins - no evidence of benefit in shortened life expectancy or in older patients (when used for secondary prevention)
- oral hypoglycaemics (OHGs) - short term risks of continuing treatment outweigh benefits – see diabetes hyperglacaemia/hypoglycaemia page
- bisphosphonates - no evidence in shortened life expectancy, unless used for hypercalcaemia due to malignancy or for bone pain

- complementary alternative medicines (CAMs) - no evidence of benefit, unless treating a low blood plasma concentration, or to treat a symptom (zinc for taste disturbance)
- proton pump inhibitors (PPIs) - determine indication for use, as this is often not clear. Continue use if patient is on long term steroid treatment, has a history of peptic ulcer disease, active bleeding, or GORD
- cancer directed therapies - often continued in many palliative patients to improve symptoms and quality of life (e.g. preventing tumour flare at the end-of-life)

Palliative care emergencies

Haemorrhage

Haemorrhage is distressing for all concerned and should be treated with urgency.

- in many situations, the sight of blood is indicative of impending death and many patients and families experience a significant increase in anxiety - use red towels if possible
- staff are often alarmed by haemorrhage, as they often feel helpless to 'do' anything to prevent it
- anticipation of bleeding is sometimes possible and can be discussed with the patient and family

Management

If the patient has been taking warfarin stop it and consider reversal with fresh frozen plasma or vitamin K. If taking other anticoagulants e.g. enoxaparin or dabigatran stop them; consult a haematologist as not reversed by vitamin K.

Haemoptysis/ENT cancers

- mild
  - reassurance
- moderate
  - radiotherapy
  - bronchoscopy if appropriate
  - laser treatment if appropriate
- severe and rapid
  - subcut midazolam and/or morphine
  - have someone stay with the patient
- severe and slower
  - suction if appropriate
  - physical touch (reassures patient)
  - drugs as for severe and rapid
- other drug therapy
  - tranexamic acid 1 to 1.5 g po 2 to 4 times daily (inhibits plasminogen activation and fibrinolysis)
  - sucralfate for oral bleeding

Upper gastro-intestinal tract

- minimise causes e.g. discontinue NSAIDs
- treat gastritis and peptic ulceration
  - drug therapy (perhaps parenterally)
    - proton pump inhibitor e.g. pantoprazole
    - H2 antagonist e.g. ranitidine
- radiotherapy and/or surgery may be appropriate

Lower gastro-intestinal tract

- radiotherapy and/or surgery may be appropriate
- drug therapy
  - tranexamic acid rectally
  - rectal steroids e.g. hydrocortisone rectal foam

Haematuria

- may occur with infection so check and treat if appropriate
- radiotherapy may help if tumour is present in the urinary tract
- endoscopic surgery may be appropriate
- drug therapy
  - tranexamic acid orally (as before)

Vaginal

- often due to infection so treat with antifungals and/or antibiotics
- palliative radiotherapy may help

Spinal cord compression

This is a relatively uncommon problem that requires urgent and effective management.

- it is one of the true medical emergencies in palliative care
- once paralysed 95% will not walk again

Symptoms

- pain (usually before neurological symptoms)
- weakness especially of lower limbs
- sensory disturbance
- loss of sphincter control

Management

- urgent assessment
  - history and clinical findings
  - MRI examination
- referral to radiation oncology is usually most appropriate
- as soon as the diagnosis is made or suspected
  - dexamethasone 16 mg daily, for a few days then tapered down according to symptom response
  - radiation therapy should be given concurrently

Decompressive laminectomy is rarely undertaken but should be considered as an option.

Miscellaneous

Diabetes, hyperglycaemia and hypoglycaemia

The pathophysiology of diabetes in the palliative care setting (and particularly in the terminal phase) may be complex as the control of blood sugar may be lost due to insulin resistance associated with illness and also because of erratic nutritional intake.

- certain malignancies e.g. pancreatic cancer also affect the beta cells directly
- control of blood glucose concentrations is important in palliative care as both hyperglycaemia and hypoglycaemia may cause symptoms resulting in a loss in the quality of life
  - e.g. marked hyperglycaemia may exacerbate pre-existing cachexia - in the catabolic state insulin has an anabolic effect
- management must balance treatment tolerability (including tolerability of blood glucose monitoring if required) with treatment efficacy and symptom control

Diabetes

Type 2 diabetes (previously called non insulin dependent diabetes [NIDDM])

- tight control of blood glucose concentrations is not necessary, although if it is easily achievable it may increase quality of life
- relax usual dietary restrictions and adjust insulin/hypoglycaemic agent use as appropriate
- if the patient is taking metformin consider discontinuing it to avoid the adverse effects of metformin e.g. nausea, weight loss and lactic acidosis. There may be a need to add a different drug e.g. insulin
- if the patient is taking a dipeptidyl peptidase inhibitor e.g. sitagliptin this may be continued but other 'third line' antidiabetic agents can be discontinued e.g. pioglitazone, dapagliflozin, acarbose
- weight loss reduces blood glucose concentrations so requirements for antidiabetic agents may reduce as weight is lost
  - once weight loss begins or appetite decreases, halve the dose of antidiabetic agent in previously well controlled patients
  - reduce doses further or stop as required
- on admission to a hospice, oral hypoglycaemic agents i.e. sulphonylureas will not be required unless there is an infection or other serious stress in which case
  - monitor blood glucose concentrations every 2 days (after the main meal if possible) and treat hyperglycaemia if symptomatic
- symptoms of hyperglycaemia will usually appear at blood glucose concentrations of > 15 mmol/L so treatment should begin only above this concentration (in the near terminal phase, may consider treatment if blood glucose > 20-25 mmol/L)
  - avoid HYPOGLYCAEMIA during this treatment as it may be difficult to reverse without systemic therapy especially if the patient is vomiting or not eating

- give a fast acting insulin analogue e.g. lispro (Humalog™), aspart (NovoRapid™) or glulisine (Apidra™) insulin 2 to 4 hourly initially (usually for 24 hours) in doses determined by monitoring - usually 5 to 10 units BUT tailor dose to both the size of the patient and food intake
- once in the range 10 to 15 mmol/L convert to an intermediate or long acting insulin e.g. isophane insulin (Protaphane™) or glargine (Lantus™) once or twice daily injections at 75% of the 24 hour short acting dose. Chart a fast acting insulin analogue e.g. lispro (Humalog™) or glulisine (Apidra™) insulin to be used for breakthrough hyperglycaemia (post-prandially if eating).
- monitor fasting blood glucose concentrations daily for several days then twice per week
- discuss management with the patient to avoid misinterpretation

Type 1 diabetes (previously called insulin dependent diabetes [IDDM]) – these are the minority of patients who are on insulin.

- insulin must be continued even in the terminally ill to avoid diabetic ketoacidosis. Consider capillary beta hydroxyl-butyrate monitoring if > 1.2 mmol/L ketosis is likely and should be treated if appropriate
- tight control is not necessary
  - a blood glucose concentration of 10 to 15 mmol/L is a good target unless patient is symptomatic
- if the patient is well nourished and has a steady oral intake negotiate with the patient (or substitute decision-maker) re the following
  - maintain the usual dose of insulin
  - monitor blood glucose concentrations twice a day every 3 days
  - when appetite decreases, increase blood glucose concentration monitoring and decrease insulin
- if patient is vomiting, is no longer eating or has a variable appetite
  - use a base line long acting insulin e.g. glargine (Lantus™) daily and chart a fast acting insulin analogue e.g. lispro (Humalog™) or glulisine (Apidra™) insulin to be used for breakthrough hyperglycaemia (post-prandially if eating)
  - monitor frequently
- if the patient is near to death
  - discuss continuation of insulin with patient and family

Hyperglycaemia

Symptoms

- at blood glucose concentrations of < 15 mmol/L
  - major symptoms are rare
- at blood glucose concentrations of 15 to 40 mmol/L
  - dehydration, dry mouth
  - thirst
  - polyuria
  - lethargy
  - blurred vision

- candidiasis
  - skin infection
  - confusion
- at blood glucose concentrations of > 40 mmol/L
  - drowsiness
  - obtundation
  - coma

NB Some of these symptoms may be present in terminally ill patients in the absence of high blood glucose concentrations.

Causes

- in diabetic patients
  - lack of insulin or hypoglycaemic agent
  - loss of dietary control
  - stress, illness
  - infection
  - myocardial infarction
  - GI motility disorders and obstruction
- in non-diabetic patients
  - malignant disease
    - > over 1/3rd of cancer patients will develop Type 2 diabetes (NIDDM) - an effect on metabolism
- drugs (even in non-diabetic patients)
  - corticosteroids e.g. dexamethasone, prednisone
  - diuretics (at high dose) e.g. bendrofluazide, frusemide

Management

- in active palliative care patients
  - closely monitor blood glucose concentrations as this may help them to retain function
- in patients who are close to death
- aim for minimal monitoring and maximal comfort
  - treat the patient rather than blood glucose concentration
  - aim for maximum quality of life by loosening control of blood glucose and encouraging eating if appropriate
- in Type 2 diabetes (non-insulin dependent) patients
  - often rehydration will partially reverse hyperglycaemia
  - BUT insulin (often only once a day) may be necessary
- in Type 1 diabetes (insulin dependent) patients
  - give insulin at least twice a day (continue with patient's usual regimen if possible) basing the dose on body weight and predicted carbohydrate intake
  - withdrawal of insulin in these patients will lead to diabetic ketoacidosis (acidosis, shock then death), often over a period of hours or days

    - if diabetic ketoacidosis occurs treat with rehydration and iv insulin if appropriate
- drug related monitoring of blood glucose
    - corticosteroids e.g. dexamethasone, prednisone
        - often cause hyperglycaemia
        - any patient who has taken them for longer than 3 weeks should have intermittent blood glucose concentration monitoring
        - diabetic patients taking them should have more intense blood glucose monitoring depending on the prognosis
            - monitor fasting blood glucose concentrations daily for a week then 3 times a week for 3 weeks or until stable then weekly
            - in terminal patients take a fasting blood glucose concentration every 2 days for one week and then according to clinical status

Hypoglycaemia

Symptoms - CNS

- behaviour changes, anxiety, aggression
- confusion
- fatigue
- seizures
- loss of consciousness

Symptoms - peripheral

- palpitations
- tremor
- sweating
- hunger
- paraesthesia
- pallor
- increased heart rate

Causes

- diseases
    - insulinomas (rare)
    - autoimmune disease (rare)
    - infection (sepsis)
    - carcinoid (rare)
- failure to adhere to good glucose monitoring technique
- organ failure
    - renal, hepatic, cardiac
- diet - low food intake
- drugs
    - insulin

- hypoglycaemic agents e.g. glipizide
- alcohol
- quinine
- pentamidine

Management

- treat/remove causes where possible
- give glucose (oral or iv), glucagon
- monitor blood glucose concentrations

Using steroids

Steroids are often seen as cure-all/miracle drugs in palliative care. Careful consideration should be given to initiating these drugs as they have many adverse effects. Most of the use in palliative care is for unlicensed and/or non-evidence based indications e.g. spinal cord compression, nerve compression, dyspnoea (from a number of causes), SVC obstruction and inflammation following radiation therapy, pain relief, anti-cancer hormone therapy, appetite stimulation and the enhancement of wellbeing.

Adverse effects

- diabetes mellitus
- osteoporosis
- avascular bone necrosis
- mental disturbances
  - insomnia, paranoid psychosis, depression, euphoria
- muscle wasting (predominantly proximal myopathy)
- peptic ulceration - not as severe as NSAID induced ulceration but of concern particularly in the elderly or patients with other risk factors
- skin thinning
- immunosuppression
  - infection - candidiasis, septicaemia
  - poor wound healing
- sodium and water retention - leading to oedema
- potassium loss
- hypertension
- Cushing's syndrome
  - moon-like face
  - striae
  - acne

Prescribing

- a trial of 5 days at 4 to 16 mg dexamethasone (dose dependent on indication) should be considered after benefit/risk has been assessed and discussed
  - dexamethasone is the preferred drug - prescribe as a single or 2 morning doses (before noon) to avoid sleep disturbance
- consider gastric protection with a PPI e.g. pantoprazole particularly in the elderly
- consider blood glucose monitoring (particularly if continuing)
- higher doses may be required if the patient is taking CYP enzyme inducers e.g. phenytoin and lower doses with inhibitors e.g. fluconazole
- withdraw completely if used for less than 2 weeks and < 6 mg dexamethasone. Otherwise tail off by 2 mg every 5 to 7 days until 2 mg once daily, then by 0.5 mg every 5 to 7 days

The last days or hours

Recognising the ending of a life may seem relatively easy or obvious but in practice the 'diagnosis of dying' may be challenging for individuals or teams. Signs may include:

- the patient becoming increasingly weak, sleepy, disinterested in getting out of bed, seeing anyone other than close family, less interested in surroundings, confused or agitated
- symptoms becoming more apparent and physical changes suggesting the body closing down becoming more noticeable (skin colour changes, skin temperature changes, slowing of respiration or Cheyne-Stokes respiration, involuntary twitching or moaning)

Management

- planning for the death is important
- if in an institution ensure that advance care plans indicate that the person is not for resuscitation
- ensure cultural or religious wishes are known and followed
- ensure that the patient and family are aware of the progression of disease and let them know what you expect to happen
- much anxiety near the end-of-life is engendered by a fear of the unknown so provide information about those things that are known to mitigate feelings of uncertainty
- anticipate what might happen rather than wait for a crisis
- anticipatory prescribing is considered to be best practice - analgesics, antiemetics, anxiolytics and antisecretory drugs should all be considered remembering that the oral route will probably be lost so use the subcut route

Common symptoms

Pain (see pain section)

opioids are the predominant analgesics used

- if the oral route is not feasible then consider
- fentanyl patches - not suitable for unstable pain but may be useful as an alternative to oral analgesic

- subcut boluses prn or continuous infusion
- conversion from oral to subcut is 2:1 for morphine and oxycodone i.e. 10 mg oral = 5m g subcut

Nausea/vomiting (see nausea/vomiting section)

- not usually a great problem unless there is intestinal obstruction or it has previously not been controlled

Agitation/distress/anxiety (see fear, anxiety, delirium sections)

Non-pharmacological management

- if there are fears/worries/tensions/spiritual issues consider what has helped in the past
- consider and address constipation/urinary retention/pain

Oral/buccal drugs

- lorazepam tablets 0.5 mg to 1 mg bd
- clonazepam drops (2.5 mg/mL - 0.1 mg per drop)
- midazolam sublingually or buccally (between gum and cheek)

Subcutaneous drugs

- midazolam 10 mg over 24hrs is a usual starting dose if not on benzodiazepine previously
- clonazepam boluses may be useful

Confusion (see delirium section)

Non-pharmacological management

- look for reversible causes
- aim for minimal disruption and have familiar people in the room

Oral drugs

- haloperidol drops (2 mg/mL - 0.1 mg per drop), initiate at 1 to 2 mg prn and titrate to response (much higher doses may be required - see haloperidol page)
- in frail or elderly patients an initial dose of 0.5 to 1 mg prn may be sufficient

Subcutaneous drugs

- haloperidol by continuous infusion 1 to 10 mg over 24 hours
- boluses of 1 to 2 mg may also be used

Excess secretions (see 'Excessive (retained) secretions' p. 47)

Non-pharmacological management

- consider position change
- it may be distressing to the family/carers rather than the patient

Drugs

- glycopyrrolate 0.6-1.2 mg subcut over 24 hours as a starting dose may help (may increase to 2.4 mg)

- hyoscine (Scopaderm™) patch may be applied behind the ear although confusion and other anticholinergic side effects may occur
- hyoscine butylbromide may be useful 20 mg subcut followed by 30 to 60 mg by continuous subcutaneous infusion over 24 hours
- secretions may become thickened and plugs may form

After death review

It can be helpful for teams to review what happened in order to learn from each patient and family.

- What things went well? What lessons have been learned that can be carried to the next person and family?
- Did the patient and family resolve all unfinished business?
- Were all opportunities to say goodbye taken?
- Was death peaceful and dignified?
- Was everything possible done to care for the family and friends?
- How could care have been improved?
- How does each of the team of professional carers feel?

Palliative chemotherapy

- palliative (i.e. non-curatative) active treatments include surgery, chemotherapy and radiotherapy
- monoclonal antibody and immunotherapy drugs are being used more commonly with effect
- signal transduction inhibitors are also being used for longer (such as EGFR, BRAF, BCR-ABL, HER2 and ALK inhibitors)
- two thirds of all chemotherapy treatments given are with 'palliative' intent
- the aim is the palliation of symptoms but the benefit of treatment should exceed the adverse effect on quality of life
- patients of all ages who present late with chemoresponsive tumours may benefit from chemotherapy
- a few patients will gain improved survival while others may get symptom relief or time to prepare for death
- patients need to be carefully supported medically, especially if frail at the time of treatment
- although doctors may be reluctant to give chemotherapy to very ill patients, patients are often keen to try it, even if the benefits may be small

Benefits

- an often only modest survival gain of months
- chemotherapy-induced symptoms are less disruptive to quality of life than the effects of the cancer itself
- may also improve the patient and their family's psychological wellbeing because 'something is being done'
- decreased tumour bulk

Adverse effects

- terminal cancer patients who receive chemotherapy during the last months of their lives are less likely to die where they wish and are more likely to undergo invasive medical procedures
- patients may express more concern about chemotherapy-induced symptoms than about the ultimate effect of the cancer
- bone marrow failure (anaemia, neutropenia, thrombocytopenia)
- unrealistic hope
- avoidance of 'death talks' and preparations
- nausea/vomiting
- lethargy/fatigue
- mucosistis and loss of taste
- peripheral neuropathies e.g. with vincristine
- alopecia
- diarrhoea
- constipation
- stomatitis

Complementary and alternative medicine

- There is no universally agreed definition of Complementary and Alternative Medicines (CAM) but The World Health Organisation defines it as:
- 'A broad set of health care practices that are not part of a country's own tradition and not integrated into the dominant health care system.' Other terms sometimes used to describe these health care practices include 'natural medicine', 'non-conventional medicine' and 'holistic medicine'.
- Complementary and Alternative Medicines (CAM) are widely used in Australasia
- a drug history should include all medicines including CAMs
- CAMs can sometimes adversely impact on conventional therapies
- CAMs use may be influenced by cultural beliefs and behaviours

Health professionals unfamiliar with CAM therapies that their patients are taking should seek information from a drug information pharmacist.

Psychosocial/spirituality

Quality of life

The primary goal of palliative care is to optimise the quality of life for patients and their families by preventing problems, delaying their onset and reducing their severity. There are many views on the nature of quality of life but one enduring view by Calman in 1984 (see 'Further reading') is that quality of life 'can be defined as subjective well-being reflecting differences or gaps between hopes and expectations and current experiences.'.

The aim of care near the end-of-life is to

- provide 'appropriate' palliative care
- provide and maintain improvement in patients' quality of life
- achieve a 'good death' for the patient and family

However, health professionals and patients often have different views on what aspects of disease and treatment are important. There are many 'expert-derived' tools available such as:

- McGill Quality of Life questionnaire
- Schedule for the Evaluation of Individual Quality of Life (SEIQoL)
- Missoula-VITAS quality of life index - encompasses a number of domains and is user-friendly (npcrc.org/files/news/missoula_vitas_quality_of_life_index.pdf). It contains questions about
  - symptoms - the level of physical discomfort and distress
  - function - perceived ability to perform accustomed functions and activities of daily living and the emotional response, experienced in relation to expectations
  - interpersonal aspects - degree of investment in personal relationships and the perceived quality of one's relations/interactions with family and friends
  - well-being - the individual's internal condition i.e. a sense of wellness or unease, contentment or lack of contentment
  - transcendent - degree of connection with an enduring construct, and of a meaning and purpose

It has also been suggested that there are a number of developmental milestones to be reached near the end-of-life that are helpful for practitioners and patients alike to recognise including:

- a sense of completion of worldly affairs, of relationships with the community and family and friends
- a sense of meaning about our own life and life in general
- an experience of love of self and others
- an acceptance of the finality of life – of one's existence
- a sense of a new self (personhood) beyond personal loss
- a surrender to the transcendent, to the unknown – letting go

Spirituality

Part of the 'task of dying' is to address spiritual concerns. Spiritual and existential concerns are important for most people at end-of-life. Spirituality should be routinely assessed, documented and addressed just as other elements of the patient's care are. Spiritual concerns may influence other symptoms. Spiritual care needs to be patient-led and should be a normal part of history taking and care plans at end-of-life.

- there is no universally agreed definition of spirituality. It includes the existential to the religious, means different things to different people and may involve a search for: ultimate beliefs/values; a sense of meaning/purpose in life; a sense of connectedness; identity and awareness; and for some people, faith and religion. Another suggestion is that 'spirituality is the way individuals seek and express meaning and purpose and experience their connectedness to the moment, to self, to others, to nature, to mortality and to the significant or sacred'
- spirituality is individually determined and culturally varied
- spiritual paths include nature (garden, sea, wilderness), relationships (self, family, friends, God), aesthetic pursuits (art, poetry, music), metaphysical pursuits (silence, prayer, ritual, philosophy)
- spiritual distress/pain is that caused by the threats to the extinction of the being/ person and their meaning of 'self'. It is a similar construct to demoralisation, but not to clinical depression
- there is some agreement that religion and spirituality are different but related concepts, with religion being within the broader category of spirituality although religion has become disconnected from spirituality for some

Spirituality assessment (or discernment)

The majority of seriously ill patients are likely to want their spirituality attended to, however there are a proportion who will find this intrusive. Questions that may initiate conversations are:

- 'Are you at peace?'
- 'What does your illness mean to you?'
- 'Tell me about your faith?'
- 'How is your illness challenging your relationship with your God?'
- 'You must be wondering "Why me"?'
- 'Do you have a belief in an afterlife?'
- 'What gives your life meaning?'

Alternatively, a spiritual wellbeing survey may be used, for example:

FACIT sp 12 Copyright © 2010 FACIT.org

Below is a list of statements that other people with your illness have said are important. Please circle or mark one number per line to indicate your response as it applies to the past 7 days.

	Not at all	A little bit	Some-what	Quite a bit	Very much
I feel peaceful	0	1	2	3	4
I have a reason for living	0	1	2	3	4
My life has been productive	0	1	2	3	4
I have trouble feeling peace of mind	0	1	2	3	4
I feel a sense of purpose in my life	0	1	2	3	4
I am able to reach down deep into myself for comfort	0	1	2	3	4
I feel a sense of harmony within myself	0	1	2	3	4
My life lacks meaning and purpose	0	1	2	3	4
I find comfort in my faith or spiritual beliefs	0	1	2	3	4
I find strength in my faith or spiritual beliefs	0	1	2	3	4
My illness has strengthened my faith or spiritual beliefs	0	1	2	3	4
I know that whatever happens with my illness, things will be okay	0	1	2	3	4

Dealing with spiritual distress

- a non-judgemental approach involving presence, compassion, and empathic and contemplative listening should be used
- the creation of space ('a safe place to suffer'), being with and listening to ('to be with and to bear witness'), touch and encouraging experiencing the natural and artistic worlds are useful approaches
- spiritual care is generally agreed to be the role of all those involved in care, with the need to involve a specialist as important as any other aspect of health care
- more specialised interventions include retreats, group therapy, meditation and religious rituals
- theological beliefs and conflicts should be referred to a chaplain/pastoral care worker
- ethical spiritual care is critical. Proselytizing is widely understood to be unethical

Negative effects of spirituality

Not all effects associated with spirituality in the health setting are positive. The negative aspects of spirituality are mostly to do with 'religious spirituality'. These include punishment or abandonment by God, religious pressure, guilt, stress, afterlife questions, and malign spirit visitations. The latter, and other unexplained phenomena are quite common and need to be heard compassionately. In most cases referral to a spiritual specialist is recommended

Advance care planning (ACP) and Advance directives (AD)

ACP is the process of discussion and planning for future health care in the context of anticipated deterioration of health. Not everyone will choose to participate in ACP.

Health care practitioners can become familiar with the particular legal requirements in their country, state or territory by contacting relevant guardianship authorities for up-to-date information. In Australia, each state and territory has different requirements.

Advance care planning

- involves the patient, health care professionals and family/carers
- incorporates the patient's beliefs, values, culture, preferences for care, current and anticipated medical status and treatment options
- needs a competent patient to participate
- should take place early in the course of a terminal illness but can happen at anytime
- may result in
  - a conversation and shared understanding between patient and health professionals
  - documentation of an ACP plan
  - the writing of an Advance Directive (see below)
  - the appointment of an enduring power of attorney/surrogate decision-maker
- is the articulation of wishes, preferences, values and goals
- respects personal autonomy and medical reality
- should be used to inform decision-making, even in acute medical emergencies
- should be regularly reviewed and updated – it is a flexible 'living' document
- is open to change, revision, and cancelation
- is not confined to medical issues – may include spiritual or interpersonal issues

Barriers to ACP

- it is time consuming
- advanced cognitive impairment (e.g. from dementia). Currently, fewer than 1% of those with a diagnosis of dementia are felt to have an ACP in place. The formulation of an Advanced Care Plan should be done as early as possible in the course of a dementing illness so that the affected individual retains a greater degree of capacity to enable its completion.
- there is sometimes a reluctance to discuss death and dying and the conversation may be difficult to initiate
- some patients prefer benign paternalistic medical care
- there may be an element of misinformation about the processes/rights/law

- acute/emergency interventions may not allow for consideration of the patient's history
- the 'disability paradox' - with age and emerging health disabilities (especially cognitive) there is a tendency to moderate the assertiveness of stated care wishes

Advance directive (AD) ('Living will')

- an AD is a written or oral directive/instruction about preferences for future care
- the process for completing advance directives should be raised early in the course of an illness when the patient is competent, free of undue influence and sufficiently informed
- the existence of an AD document or conversation needs to be established
- it becomes effective if the person loses capacity
- it may encompass refusal of, or consent to, a particular treatment
- there is no medical obligation or duty to provide treatments not offered, not effective or unavailable
- clinicians are obliged to give effect to an AD but in emergencies medical indications to save life may take priority (if AD not known about)
- in some states of Australia, directives are legally binding on health professionals. There may also be the provision for patients to nominate legal proxies who can make decisions on their behalf

Competency or capacity

- an individual's ability to perform a particular task at a particular point in time e.g. a decision regarding their current or future health care includes competency and capacity
- all adults are presumed to have capacity unless it is proven otherwise
- in order to demonstrate capacity, three elements must be met:
- the person is able to understand and appreciate key basic facts that are relevant to the decision to be made
- the person is able to weigh the risks and benefits of any given course of action
- the person is able to express a choice that is made in the absence of coercion
- competency may fluctuate depending on the issues under consideration
- the patient needs to be able to understand information relevant to the decision, to reason and deliberate, to retain the information (even for only a short time), to communicate by any means
- capacity does not necessarily imply rationality
- if capacity is not possessed decisions must be taken by others in that person's best interests and in the least restrictive manner possible
- Legally authorised proxy/surrogate decision-maker
- refer to guidelines available for each country, state or territory as variations in the law in different areas exist
- the preferable surrogate is a close and mature relative. It is a difficult role
- All decisions must be made with the patient's best interest in mind and tend to be conservative and life-affirming.

Testamentary Capacity

- this is the legal and mental ability to make or alter a valid will
- the testator must have knowledge of extent and value of their property, knowledge of their natural beneficiaries, and the ability to communicate this knowledge

Grief and loss

Grief is the distressing emotional response initiated by the death of a loved and attached person, or a loss. It is a normal, adjustment process. Spontaneous recovery occurs over time for the majority.

- grief begins at loss/diagnosis
- there are no specific stages of grief. Grief is never fully resolved
- modern society is death-denying and death-defying
- symptoms include sadness, anger, waves of distress, tearfulness, initial insomnia, pining, haunting reminiscences, fleeting auditory or visual pseudo-hallucinations or a sense of presence of the departed
- mourning is the behavioural responses of grieving. Culture and social norms are determinants. Mourning customs serve to organise, protect and support the grief-stricken
- grief is age-influenced. Children do not develop the capacity to appreciate the permanency of death until aged 9-10. In the elderly grief may be curtailed if the death is expected
- grief therapy may be ineffective and potentially harmful, except in distressed/ complicated grievers

Grief and loss in dementia

Dementia has been characterised as 'the long goodbye'. Due to personality changes and a decline in the ability of a person with dementia to recognise even close relatives, family members can feel as though they lost the person long before the time of their death, perhaps due to the person being perceived as physically present but psychologically absent for some years prior to death. Feelings of ambivalence and guilt are common, and the grief of a close relative of someone with dementia can occur in a vacuum of social isolation if the wider social circle of an affected family member has drifted away during their loved one's decline.

Relatives may become affected by a phenomenon known as disenfranchised grief, where their grief is not validated by others in circumstances where their relationship with the departed is not recognised and their loss unacknowledged. In a similar vein, stigma against those with dementia may lead to a disenfranchised or devalued death, where the value of the departed's very personhood is no longer acknowledged by others who might otherwise lend support.

Depression rates in family caregivers of people with dementia can be as high as 50%. The grief of dementia caregivers frequently goes unrecognised by attending health professionals.

Complicated grief

- intense and/or protracted (> 1-2 years)
- it is characterised by prolonged longing and yearning for the deceased, intrusive thoughts or images, anger, guilt, emotional numbness, avoidance of reminders and difficulties redefinition
- it occurs in 10-15% of bereaved people
- it is accompanied by increased psychological and physical morbidity, substance abuse and suicide
- risk factors include sudden, unexpected, traumatic death, pre-existing dependant or ambivalent relationship, psychological/psychiatric vulnerability, disenfranchised grief (the hidden grief of those socially unable to express their response), compounded by major depression or substance abuse

Management of grief

- 'death talk' (anticipatory grief) and advance care planning may mitigate/moderate grief
- early identification of those at high risk for bereavement follow-up
- support, empathy, normalisation, offer pragmatic information/education
- encouraging adaptation and restructuring of a world without the lost one, acknowledgement of the emotional 'scar'
- short term mild hypnotic medication if marked insomnia
- specific counselling e.g. Cognitive Behavioural Therapy if complicated grief, perhaps with antidepressant medication
- cathartic expression of distress is of minimal, if any, benefit

Pharmacopoeia

Drugs listed are preferred choices in palliative care.

Baclofen

Class: GABA derivative musculoskeletal muscle relaxant

Indications: relief of musculoskeletal spasm

Contraindications/cautions: epilepsy, subcut injection, psychosis, schizophrenia, depression, mania, GI ulceration, cerebrovascular disease, alcoholism, diabetes (may increase blood glucose concentrations), hypertension

Adverse reactions: *common* nausea, sedation, somnolence; *less common* decreased cardiac output, hypotension, GI disturbance, respiratory depression, light-headedness, personality changes, headache, insomnia, euphoria, depression, weakness, tremor, hallucinations, dry mouth, tinnitus

Metabolism/clearance: mainly excreted in urine unchanged (80%) so dose adjust in renal impairment

Interactions:

- *additive drowsiness and CNS depression* with other **CNS depressant drugs e.g. alcohol, benzodiazepines (e.g. clonazepam), opioids**
- *increased muscle relaxation* with **tricyclic antidepressants e.g. nortriptyline**

Dosing:

oral:	5 to 20 mg 3 to 4 times a day (start at 5 mg 3 times a day)
subcut:	not available

Syringe driver: only intrathecal inj available - not for subcut use

Mechanism of action: works in the spinal cord where it stimulates GABA-receptors which inhibit the release of glutamate and aspartate (excitatory). Also has CNS depressant actions.

Onset: variable - hours to weeks

Notes:

- Stopping abruptly may result in a withdrawal reaction (confusion, psychosis, tachycardia, hyperthermia and rebound spasticity).

Bisacodyl

Class: laxative - stimulant

Indications: constipation

Contraindications/cautions: acute abdominal pain, intestinal obstruction

Adverse reactions: *common* abdominal cramps, diarrhoea, perianal irritation (usually with suppositories); *less common* atonic colon (on prolonged use), hypokalaemia

Metabolism/clearance: mainly excreted in faeces

Interactions:

- *decreased clinical effects of* **antispasmodics (e.g. hyoscine butylbromide)** may occur due to stimulant effects of bisacodyl

Dosing:

oral:	5 to 10 mg at night or 5 mg twice a day
subcut:	not available
rectal:	10 mg at night

Syringe driver: not available

Mechanism of action: stimulates colonic activity via nerves in the intestinal mucosa

Onset: oral: 6 to 12 hours rectal: 20 to 60 minutes

Notes:

- May be useful in opioid induced constipation especially in combination with a softener.

Buprenorphine*

Class: analgesic - opioid, partial mu agonist/kappa antagonist

Indications: moderate to severe pain

Contraindications/cautions: buprenorphine hypersensitivity/allergy, use with other opioids, adverse effects such as respiratory depression may not completely respond to naloxone, COPD, use with benzodiazepines

Adverse reactions: *see morphine*

Metabolism/clearance: metabolised by unclear pathway

Interactions:

- *additive CNS depression* with other **CNS depressants e.g. benzodiazepines (e.g. lorazepam), phenothiazines (e.g. chlorpromazine), tricyclic antidepressants (e.g. amitriptyline), other opioids, alcohol**

Dosing:

sublingual combo:	not used
subcut:	not used
patch:	5 to 20 micrograms/hour (each patch lasts for 7 days)

Syringe driver: compatibility unknown so best to infuse on its own. Irritancy potential is unknown.

Mechanism of action: partially stimulates mu- and blocks kappa opioid receptors in the CNS and gastrointestinal tract

Peak effect: patch: 60 hours after initial application

Onset: 11 to 21 hours

Duration: patch: 7 days

Notes:

- As buprenorphine is only a partial agonist of mu receptors and an antagonist of kappa receptors it should not be used with other opioids or within 24 hours of them as it may lead to severe opioid withdrawal.
- As patches last for 7 days and peak concentrations occur at 60 hours do not use in rapidly escalating pain.
- For acute toxicity give naloxone 2 mg and repeat as required (max 10 mg) over a prolonged time but be aware that full reversal of toxicity may not occur as buprenorphine binding to opioid receptors is high.
- Do not cut patches.
- Equivalence to other opioid data are sparse but 20 micrograms/hour patch may be equivalent to 90 mg oral morphine per day.
- It is recommended that no more than two patches be applied at the same time regardless of the patch strength
- A new patch should not be applied to the same skin site for the subsequent 3 to 4 weeks

* **Drugs that are either not available or not funded in New Zealand**

Cholestyramine

Class: anion exchange resin

Indications: hypercholesterolaemia, pruritis due to partial biliary obstruction, diarrhoea associated with ileal resection or cholerrhoeic enteropathy

Contraindications/cautions: complete biliary obstruction, diabetes, nephrotic syndrome, phenylketonuria, prolonged use, constipation

Adverse reactions: *common* constipation, faecal impaction, hyperchloraemic acidosis, perianal irritation, intestinal obstruction; *less common* nausea, bloating

Metabolism/clearance: combines with bile acids and is excreted in the faeces - not absorbed

Interactions:

- *decreased clinical effect/toxicity of some drugs* (due to decreased absorption- see below)
- *altered concentrations of some drugs that undergo enterohepatic recycling*

Dosing:

oral: 4 to 16 g per day

Syringe driver: not available

Mechanism of action: binds bile acids which reduces plasma bile acid concentrations

Onset: pruritus: 4 to 7 days

Notes:

- As absorption of other drugs will be affected take all other drugs 1 hour before or 4 to 6 hours after cholestyramine. Sachet contents must be mixed with 100 to 150 mL of fluid before administering.

Citalopram

Class: Antidepressant - SSRI (Selective Serotonin Re-uptake Inhibitor)

Indications: depression, anxiety (chronic)

Contraindications/cautions: hepatic impairment, epilepsy, bleeding disorders, abrupt withdrawal

Adverse reactions: *common* nausea, sweating, tremor, diarrhoea (excessive serotonin), constipation, somnolence; *less common* dry mouth, cough, postural hypotension, tachycardia, amnesia, taste disturbance, visual disturbances, pruritus, hyponatraemia, sexual dysfunction, QT prolongation

Metabolism/clearance: metabolism unknown

Interactions:

- *additive risk of serotonin syndrome* (potentially fatal syndrome - symptoms include sweating, diarrhoea, confusion) with other serotonergic drugs **e.g. amitriptyline, carbamazepine, fluoxetine, paroxetine, tramadol, lithium**
- *increased risk of bleeding* (antiplatelet effect) with **anticoagulants**

Dosing:

oral:	10 to 40 mg once a day
subcut/rectal:	not available

Syringe driver: not available

Mechanism of action: blocks the reuptake of serotonin

Onset: depression: 2 to 4 weeks   anxiety or pain: 3 to 7 days

Peak response: 5 to 6 weeks

Notes:

- **Escitalopram** is available. Doses used are approximately half.
- Doses of greater than 40 mg per day have been associated with QT interval prolongation.

Clonazepam

Class: anticonvulsant - benzodiazepine

Indications (NB some may be unlicensed): epilepsy, convulsions, sedation, anxiety, agitation, restless leg syndrome, neuropathic pain, dyspnoea, hiccups, myoclonic jerks

Contraindications/cautions: avoid sudden withdrawal, respiratory depression

Adverse reactions: *common* fatigue, drowsiness (at higher doses); *less common* respiratory depression, incontinence, co-ordination problems, disinhibition, increase in salivation, confusion

Metabolism/clearance: metabolised by metabolising enzyme CYP3A mainly in the liver

Interactions:

- *increased clinical effect/toxicity of clonazepam* (due to increased blood concentrations) may occur with some CYP metabolising enzyme inhibitors (see above) **e.g. clarithromycin, fluconazole, grapefruit juice, itraconazole, ketoconazole**
- *decreased clinical effect/toxicity of clonazepam* (due to decreased blood concentrations) may occur with some CYP metabolism enzyme inducers (see above) **e.g. carbamazepine, phenobarbitone, phenytoin, rifampicin, St John's wort**
- *additive CNS effects* with other **CNS depressants e.g. opioids (e.g. morphine), phenothiazines (e.g. chlorpromazine), tricyclic antidepressants (e.g. amitriptyline), alcohol may occur with concomitant clonazepam**

Dosing: sedation, anxiety, agitation, restless leg syndrome, neuropathic pain, dyspnoea, hiccups, convulsions

oral:	0.5 to 8 mg a day (1 to 2 mg a day usually adequate)
subcut:	1 to 8 mg/24 hours
rectal:	not available

Syringe driver: see syringe driver compatibility table

Mechanism of action: may enhance the effect of GABA, an inhibitory neurotransmitter in the CNS

Onset: oral (seizure control): 20 to 40 minutes

Half life: > 30 hours (18 to 45 hours)

Notes:

- A long acting benzodiazepine so difficult to titrate to response.
- Benzodiazepines may reduce dyspnoea by anxiolytic and sedative effects.
- Approximate equivalent oral anxiolytic/sedative doses:

diazepam	5 mg
lorazepam	0.5 to 1 mg
clonazepam	0.5 mg
temazepam	10 mg
midazolam	7.5 mg
triazolam	0.25 mg

Pharmacological properties of benzodiazepines

Drug	Anxiolytic	Night sedation	Muscle relaxant	Anticonvulsant
diazepam	+++	+	+++	++
lorazepam	+++	++	+	+
clonazepam	++	+	+	+++
temazepam	+	+++	+	+
midazolam	+	+++	+	+++

Codeine phosphate

Class: analgesic - opioid (metabolised to morphine)

Indications (NB some may be unlicensed): step 2 in the WHO analgesic ladder, cough, diarrhoea

Contraindications/cautions: avoid use with other opioid analgesics

Adverse reactions: as for morphine - very constipating

Metabolism/clearance: metabolised by metabolising enzyme CYP2D6 mainly in the liver to an active metabolite - morphine. Minor metabolism by 3A.

Interactions:

- *decreased clinical effect/toxicity of codeine* (due to decreased blood concentrations of morphine - an active metabolite) may occur with some CYP metabolising enzyme inhibitors (see above) **e.g. bupropion, fluoxetine, paroxetine (not citalopram), quinine**
- *additive CNS effects with other* **CNS depressants e.g. benzodiazepines (e.g. lorazepam), phenothiazines (e.g. chlorpromazine), tricyclic antidepressants (e.g. amitriptyline), other opioids, alcohol** may occur with concomitant codeine
- *inhibition of the antidiarrhoeal effects of codeine* may occur with concomitant **metoclopramide/domperidone**

Dosing:

pain, cough and diarrhoea:

oral:	15 to 60 mg 4 to 6 hourly (max. 240 mg in 24 hours)
subcut:	not recommended - use other opioid instead
rectal:	not available

Syringe driver: available as injection but not used

Mechanism of action: metabolised to morphine and other active metabolites

Peak effect: 2 to 4 hours

Duration: 4 to 8 hours

Notes:

- Combination products are not recommended.
- 10% of dose is converted to morphine in "normal" metabolisers i.e. 60 mg codeine = 6 mg morphine.
- 5 to 10% of the Caucasian population may be unable to metabolise codeine to morphine.
- Combination with other opioids is illogical.
- Dihydrocodeine slow release is available although it is not often used in palliative care.

Cyclizine

Class: antiemetic - antihistaminic

Indications: nausea/vomiting (including motion sickness)

Contraindications/cautions: prostatic hypertrophy, narrow angle glaucoma

Adverse reactions: *common* drowsiness, restlessness, dry mouth, blurred vision, constipation; *less common* insomnia, hallucinations (more common in elderly), cardiac arrhythmias

Metabolism/clearance: metabolised in the liver mainly to norcyclizine

Interactions:

- *additive CNS effects* with other **CNS depressants e.g. benzodiazepines (e.g. lorazepam), phenothiazines (e.g. chlorpromazine), tricyclic antidepressants (e.g. amitriptyline), opioids, alcohol**

Dosing:

oral:	25 to 50 mg 3 times a day (cyclizine hydrochloride)
subcut:	75 to 150 mg/24 hours (cyclizine lactate) (well diluted)
rectal:	not available

Syringe driver: see syringe driver compatibility table.

Mechanism of action: acts on the histamine receptors in the vomiting centre in the CNS and has anticholinergic properties

Peak concentration: approx 2 hours

Notes:

- Although there is a theoretical interaction with prokinetic antiemetics (prokinetics stimulate the gut while cyclizine slows it down) use together is common and may be justified on the basis of central nervous system receptors antagonism.

Dexamethasone

Class: corticosteroid - glucocorticoid

Indications (NB some may be unlicensed): cerebral oedema (raised intracranial pressure), allergy/anaphylaxis, replacement, shock, collagen diseases, asthma, respiratory insufficiency, leukaemia, lymphoma, rheumatic disease, psoriasis, colitis, enteritis, hypercalcaemia of malignancy, nausea/vomiting, sweating, itch, hiccup, pain, liver capsule pain, tenesmus, increased energy, weight gain

Contraindications/cautions: infections, GI bleeding

Adverse reactions: *common* insomnia (decrease by giving as single dose in the morning); *less common* sodium/fluid retention, GI ulceration, delayed wound healing, thinning of skin (on prolonged use), muscle weakness (proximal myopathy), Cushing's syndrome, weight gain, mania, depression, delirium, hyperglycaemia, osteoporosis

Metabolism/clearance: metabolised by metabolising enzyme CYP3A (major) mainly in the liver

Interactions:

- *increased clinical effect/toxicity of dexamethasone* (due to increased blood concentrations) may occur with some CYP metabolising enzyme inhibitors (see above) **e.g. aprepitant, clarithromycin, grapefruit juice, indinavir, itraconazole, ketoconazole, nelfinavir, ritonavir, telapravir, voriconazole**
- *decreased clinical effect/toxicity of dexamethasone* (due to decreased blood concentrations) may occur with some CYP metabolising enzyme inducers (see above) **e.g. carbamazepine, phenobarbitone, phenytoin, rifampicin, St John's wort**
- *decreased clinical effect/toxicity of other drugs metabolised by CYP enzymes* (due to induction of their metabolism by dexamethasone) may occur **e.g. aprepitant, carbamazepine, clonazepam, diazepam, domperidone, fentanyl, itraconazole, ketoconazole, methadone, midazolam, prednisone, quetiapine, triazolam**
- *increased ris***k of GI bleed/ulceration** when given with NSAIDs (e.g. diclofenac)

Dosing:

oral:	4 to 32 mg in 24 hours
subcut:	4 to 16 mg/24 hours
rectal:	not available

Syringe driver: see syringe drivers BUT best given as a morning bolus by subcut injection/short infusion

Mechanism of action: decreases inflammatory response via induction of lipocortin.

Onset: 8 to 24 hours

Notes:

- Anti-inflammatory effect: 3 mg dexamethasone = 20 mg prednisone = 80 mg hydrocortisone.
- On discontinuation decrease dose slowly (taper) unless the patient has been taking it for less than 5 days in which case dose tapering is not necessary.
- Alteration in mood is not usually seen below 6 mg dexamethasone (40 mg prednisone) per day.

- Corticosteroid-induced insomnia responds to benzodiazepines (e.g. temazepam)
- Corticosteroid induced mood disorder is usually depression and rarely mania.
- The use of steroids in palliative care is common and sometimes, particularly at high dose, consideration should be given to the appropriateness of their use.
- The use of 0.5 to 1 mg dexamethasone in a syringe driver may reduce the risk of irritation at the subcutaneous site but adverse effects can occur even at low dose.

Diclofenac

Class: non-steroidal anti-inflammatory drug (NSAID)

Indications (NB some may be unlicensed): pain associated with inflammation, itch, sweating

Contraindications/cautions: GI ulceration, asthma (in sensitive patients), renal, cardiac or hepatic impairment

Adverse reactions: *common* GI ulceration (more common if elderly, on steroids or aspirin), diarrhoea, indigestion, nausea; *less common* dizziness, rash, nephrotoxicity, hepatitis, oedema, hypertension, headache, tinnitus, proctitis (rectal administration) NB inhibits platelet aggregation - may prolong bleeding time.

Metabolism/clearance: metabolised by metabolising enzyme CYP2C9 mainly in the liver

Interactions:

- *increased clinical effect/toxicity of diclofenac* (due to increased blood concentrations) may occur with some CYP metabolising enzyme inhibitors (see above) **e.g. fluconazole**
- *decreased clinical effect/toxicity of diclofenac* (due to decreased blood concentrations) may occur with some CYP metabolism enzyme inducers (see above) **e.g. phenobarbitone, phenytoin, rifampicin**
- *increased risk of renal toxicity and hyperkalaemia* with **ACE inhibitors (e.g. enalapril)**
- *increased risk of gastro-intestinal bleed* with corticosteroids (e.g. dexamethasone)
- *increased clinical effect/toxicity* of **lithium, digoxin, methotrexate, warfarin** may occur with concomitant diclofenac so monitor
- *decreased clinical effects* of **diuretics (e.g. furosemide), antihypertensives (e.g. propranolol)** may occur with concomitant diclofenac

Dosing:

oral:	50 to 150 mg per day in 3 divided doses for normal release and 2 divided doses (sometimes just 1) for long acting preparations.
subcut:	inj available but not for subcut injection as too irritant
rectal:	as for normal release oral

Syringe driver: not recommended

Mechanism of action: inhibits prostaglandin synthesis - prostaglandins are involved in inflammation and pain

Peak effect: oral (normal release): 0.3 to 2 hours

Duration: oral (normal release): 6 to 8 hours

Notes:

- Co-analgesic often used with opioids in bone and soft tissue pain.
- NSAID of choice in palliative care.
- Patients at risk of gastro-intestinal bleeds should be prescribed gastric protection (e.g. pantoprazole) prophylactically.

Docusate

Class: laxative - faecal softener

Indications: constipation

Contraindications/cautions: acute abdominal pain

Adverse reactions: *less common* abdominal cramps, atonic colon (on prolonged use), bitter taste

Metabolism/clearance: absorbed from the gastrointestinal tract and excreted mainly in the bile

Interactions:

- *decreased clinical effect* of **antispasmodics (e.g. hyoscine butylbromide)** may occur with concomitant docusate

Dosing:

oral:	100 to 480 mg daily (with senna 1 to 2 tabs at night - max 4 tabs)
subcut:	not available
rectal:	1 as required

Syringe driver: not available

Mechanism of action: thought to increase intestinal secretions and facilitate their movement into faeces producing softer stools

Onset: oral :1 to 3 days

Notes:

- As docusate has some stimulant action it should be avoided in complete intestinal obstruction, as should all stimulant laxatives.
- Not laxative of choice in opioid induced constipation as a single agent but useful in combination with a stimulant (e.g. Laxsol™) although giving a softener and a stimulant as separate tablets may be more effective.

Domperidone

Class: antiemetic - prokinetic, dopamine antagonist

Indications: dyspeptic symptom complex including gastro-oesophageal reflux oesophagitis, epigastric sense of fullness, feeling of abdominal distension, upper abdominal pain, eructation, flatulence and heartburn, nausea, vomiting

Contraindications/cautions: complete intestinal obstruction

Adverse reactions: *common* hyperprolactinaemia, breast tenderness, QT prolongation; *less common* abdominal cramps, diarrhoea, dry mouth, headache, dizziness

Metabolism/clearance: metabolised by metabolising enzyme CYP3A mainly in the liver and gut

Interactions:

- *increased clinical effect/toxicity of domperidone* (due to increased blood concentrations) may occur with some CYP metabolising enzyme inhibitors (see above) **e.g. aprepitant, clarithromycin, grapefruit juice, indinavir, itraconazole, ketoconazole, nelfinavir, ritonavir, telapravir, voriconazole**
- *decreased clinical effect/toxicity of domperidone* (due to decreased blood concentrations) may occur with some CYP metabolising enzyme inducers (see above) **e.g. carbamazepine, phenobarbitone, phenytoin, rifampicin, St John's wort**
- *decreased prokinetic effect of domperidone* may occur with **anticholinergic drugs (e.g. amitriptyline, hyoscine)**
- *additive increased risk of QT interval prolongation* (cardiac adverse effect which may lead to arrhythmias) with **tricyclic antidepressants (e.g. amitriptyline), flecainide, erythromycin, theophylline, methotrimeprazine (levomepromazine)**

Dosing:

oral:	10 mg 3 times a day
subcut:	not available
rectal:	10 mg supp available

Syringe driver: not available

Mechanism of action: similar to metoclopramide - blocks dopamine receptors in the upper gastrointestinal tract, chemo-receptor trigger zone (CTZ) and the CNS (minimal effect on CNS therefore less likely to cause extrapyramidal side effects than metoclopramide)

Peak concentration: 30 to 110 minutes

Notes:

- Main advantage over metoclopramide is less extrapyramidal side effects but not available in injectable form.
- Useful in nausea and vomiting associated with gastric stasis.
- The United States Federal Drug Agency has warned of domperidone induced QT interval prolongation and recommend a maximum of 30 mg in 24 hours. A risk benefit assessment should be carried out when higher doses are considered along with a baseline QT interval assessment.

Duloxetine*

Class: serotonin and noradrenaline reuptake inhibitor antidepressant

Indications (NB some may be unlicensed): depression, anxiety, neuropathic pain

Contraindications/cautions: concurrent MAOI, hepatic failure, raised ocular pressure, severe renal impairment

Adverse reactions: *common* insomnia, sweating, fatigue, nausea, dry mouth, diarrhoea, palpitations, blurred vision, hypotension, syncope; *less common* mydriasis, suicidal ideation, hepatotoxicity, hyponatraemia, serotonin syndrome, tachycardia, dizziness, tinnitus

Metabolism/clearance: Metabolised by CYP1A2 and 2D6

Interactions:

- *increased clinical effect/toxicity of duloxetine** (due to increased blood concentrations) may occur with some CYP metabolising enzyme inhibitors (see above) **e.g. bupropion, paroxetine (not citalopram), quinine, ciprofloxacin, ketoconazole**
- *decreased clinical effect/toxicity of duloxetine** (due to decreased blood concentrations) may occur with some CYP metabolising enzyme inducers (see above) **e.g. phenobarbitone, phenytoin, rifampicin, cruciferous vegetables, smoking, barbecued food**
- *additive risk of serotonin syndrome* (potentially fatal syndrome - symptoms include sweating, diarrhoea, confusion) with other serotonergic drugs **e.g. carbamazepine, citalopram, tricyclic antidepressants (e.g. amitriptyline), lithium, tramadol** interacts with excessive **alcohol** *to cause hepatic injury*

Dosing:

depression	oral:	60 mg/day
anxiety	oral:	30 mg to 120 mg/day
neuropathic pain	oral:	60 mg to 120 mg/day
subcut:	not available	
rectal:	not available	

Syringe driver: not available

Mechanism of action: increases available noradrenaline and serotonin in the CNS

* **Drugs that are either not available or not funded in New Zealand**

Enoxaparin

Class: anticoagulant - low molecular weight heparin

Indications: prophylaxis of venous thromboembolic disease post-op and bedridden patients.
Treatment of venous thromboembolic disease, unstable angina and myocardial infarction.
Prevention of thrombus during haemodialysis, duration of more than 30 days treatment

Contraindications/cautions: heparin allergy, active bleeding, recent haemorrhagic stroke, low platelets, renal impairment (adjust dose), spinal/epidural medication, prosthetic heart valve, history of gastrointestinal ulceration/bleed

Adverse reactions: *common* haemorrhage, haematoma, elevated LFTs; *less common* allergic reactions, skin necrosis, thrombocytopenia

Metabolism/clearance: metabolised but cleared mainly by the kidneys so adjust dose in renal failure

Interactions:

- *increased effect of enoxaparin* may occur with **other drugs that decrease blood clotting e.g. aspirin, clopidogrel, warfarin, heparin**
- *increased risk of bleeding* when combined with **NSAIDs e.g. diclofenac**
- *decreased effect of enoxaparin* may occur with **haemostats e.g. tranexamic acid, phytomenadione (vitamin K)**

Dosing:

oral:	not available
subcut:	treatment (of DVT etc): 1.5 mg/kg once a day or 1 mg/kg twice a day (lower in the obese and renal failure patients)
prophylaxis:	20 to 40 mg once or twice a day

Syringe driver: not available

Mechanism of action: has high anti-Xa activity

Peak anti-Xa activity: 3 to 5 hours post inj

Notes:

- As the coagulation ability of cancer patients is altered it may be that low molecular weight heparins are a better choice in these patients than oral anticoagulants.

Fentanyl

Class: analgesic - opioid

Indications: step 3 on the WHO ladder for severe pain, anaesthetic premed

Contraindications/cautions: fentanyl hypersensitivity/allergy (not nausea/ hallucinations)

Adverse reactions: *see morphine* - less constipating (reduce dose of laxatives when converting from morphine), perhaps less sedating and less emetogenic than other opioids

Metabolism/clearance: metabolised by metabolising enzyme CYP3A mainly in the liver

Interactions:

- *increased clinical effect/toxicity of fentanyl* (due to increased blood concentrations) may occur with some CYP metabolising enzyme inhibitors (see above) **e.g. aprepitant, clarithromycin, grapefruit juice, indinavir, itraconazole, ketoconazole, nelfinavir, ritonavir, telapravir, voriconazole**
- *decreased clinical effect/toxicity of fentanyl* (due to decreased blood concentrations) may occur with some CYP metabolism enzyme inducers (see above) **e.g. carbamazepine, phenobarbitone, phenytoin, rifampicin, St John's wort**
- *additive CNS depression* with other CNS depressants **e.g. benzodiazepines (e.g. lorazepam), phenothiazines (e.g. chlorpromazine), tricyclic antidepressants (e.g. amitriptyline), other opioids, alcohol**

Dosing:

subcut:	50 to 300 micrograms in 24 hours initially
patch:	12.5 to 300 micrograms/hour (each patch lasts for 3 days)

Syringe driver: see syringe driver compatibility table

Mechanism of action: stimulates opioid receptors in the CNS and gastrointestinal tract

Peak effect: patch: 12 to 24 hours after initial application

Duration: patch: 72 hours (plus depot effect see later)

Notes:

- Patches are unsuitable for opioid naïve patients.
- If patient is hot, or there is a heat pad near the patch, rate of absorption may increase
- If patch comes unstuck use Micropore™ round edges to reattach.
- For acute toxicity give naloxone 2 mg and repeat as required (max 10 mg) over a prolonged time (depot in skin - see below).
- Patches leave a depot in the skin which will carry on releasing fentanyl after removal (at least 17 hours for concentrations to drop by 50%).
- Dose adjustments should usually be done every 3 days.
- Use another opioid or the fentanyl injection subcut/sublingual/intranasal for breakthrough - for fentanyl the dose may not relate to background so start at 25 micrograms fentanyl and titrate to effect.

continued

- Approximate conversion is morphine (po): fentanyl (subcut/patch) = 150:1 i.e. 10 mg morphine po = 66 micrograms fentanyl subcut but in chronic use this can only be used as an estimate.

Conversion Chart:

Oral morphine	fentanyl patch
(mg/24 hours)	**(mcg/hour)**
<60	12.5
60-134	25
135-224	50
225-314	75
315-404	100
405-494	125
495-584	150
585-674	175
675-764	200
765-854	225
855-944	250
945-1,034	275
1,035-1,124	300

Fluconazole

Class: antifungal - triazole

Indications: fungal infections – cryptococcosis, candidiasis, prophylaxis, dermatomycoses

Contraindications/cautions: renal impairment, hepatic impairment

Adverse reactions: *common* gastrointestinal upset, headache; *less common* rash (discontinue), blood disorders, arrhythmias, dizziness, convulsions, hypokalaemia

Metabolism/clearance: mainly excreted by the kidneys (fraction excreted by the kidneys unchanged = 0.8) so care in renal failure

Interactions:

- *increased clinical effect/toxicity* of some drugs (see below) (due to increased blood concentrations of them) may occur due to inhibition of metabolising enzymes by fluconazole **e.g. diazepam, diclofenac, gliclazide, ibuprofen, indomethacin, lansoprazole, naproxen, omeprazole, pantoprazole, phenytoin, warfarin**
- *decreased clinical effect* of **amphotericin** may occur with concomitant fluconazole

Dosing:

oral:

vaginal candidiasis	150 mg as a single dose
cryptococcal infections/systemic candidiasis	200 to 400 mg once a day for 7 days
oropharyngeal candidiasis	50 to 100 mg once a day for 7 days
prophylaxis in malignancy	50 mg once a day

subcut: not usually used subcut, iv: refer to package insert

rectal: not available

Syringe driver: not applicable

Mechanism of action: inhibits fungal cell membrane formation

Notes:

- Useful in severe or recurrent fungal infections.
- May be less likely to interact with other CYP metabolised drugs (see above) than ketoconazole.

Fluoxetine

Class: antidepressant - SSRI (Selective Serotonin Re-uptake Inhibitor)

Indications (NB some may be unlicensed): depression and associated anxiety, bulimia nervosa, obsessive-compulsive disorder, premenstrual dysphoric disorder, neuropathic pain

Contraindications/cautions: epilepsy, bleeding disorders (decreases platelet aggregation)

Adverse reactions: *common* nausea, sweating, tremor, diarrhoea (excessive serotonin), taste disturbance, sexual dysfunction; *less common* dry mouth, cough, constipation, postural hypotension, tachycardia, somnolence, amnesia, visual disturbances, pruritus, hyponatraemia

Metabolism/clearance: metabolised by metabolising enzyme CYP2D6 mainly in the liver

Interactions:

- *increased clinical effect/toxicity of fluoxetine* (due to increased blood concentrations) may occur with some CYP metabolising enzyme inhibitors (see above) **e.g. bupropion, paroxetine (not citalopram), quinine**
- *increased clinical effect/toxicity of some drugs* (due to increased blood concentrations of them) may occur with fluoxetine due to metabolising enzyme inhibition by fluoxetine **e.g. amitriptyline, codeine** (decreased morphine concentrations so decreased clinical efficacy of codeine), **haloperidol, metoclopramide, nortriptyline, promethazine, tamoxifen** (decreased endoxifen (active metabolite) concentrations so decreased clinical effects)
- *additive risk of serotonin syndrome* (potentially fatal syndrome - symptoms include sweating, diarrhoea, confusion) with other serotonergic drugs **e.g. carbamazepine, citalopram, tricyclic antidepressants (e.g. amitriptyline), lithium, tramadol**

Dosing:

oral:	20 to 80 mg in the morning
subcut:	not available
rectal:	not available

Syringe driver: not available

Mechanism of action: blocks the reuptake of serotonin, a neurotransmitter, in the CNS

Onset: depression/anxiety: 2 to 4 weeks pain: 3 to 7 days

Peak response: 5 to 6 weeks

Notes:

- Fluoxetine has a half life of 48 hours but its active metabolite (norfluoxetine) has a half life of 11 days.
- Watch for serotonin syndrome if switching antidepressants as it takes four to five half lives to clear a drug from the body i.e. 44 to 55 days for fluoxetine/norfluoxetine.
- Withdrawal symptoms on stopping fluoxetine are unlikely to occur.
- Tablets are dispersible in water allowing dosing increments of < 20 mg. Capsule contents are also dispersible in water.

Gabapentin

Class: anticonvulsant

Indications (NB some may be unlicensed): partial seizures, including secondarily generalised tonic-clonic seizures, initially as add-on therapy in patients who have not achieved adequate control with standard antiepileptic drugs, neuropathic pain, insomnia

Contraindications/cautions: renal disease (reduce dose), absence seizures, encephalopathy

Adverse reactions: *common* easy bruising (purpura), increased blood pressure, dizziness, ataxia, somnolence, blurred vision; *less common* fatigue, headache, anxiety, GI effects, sexual dysfunction, oedema, twitching, tremor, confusion, suicidal thoughts

Metabolism/clearance: not metabolised, mainly excreted unchanged by the kidneys (fraction excreted unchanged by the kidney = 0.8) so care and adjust dose in renal dysfunction

Interactions:

- *decreased clinical effect/toxicity of gabapentin* with antacids **e.g. Mylanta P™** due to decreased absorption of gabapentin
- *additive CNS depression* with other CNS depressants **e.g. benzodiazepines (e.g. lorazepam), phenothiazines (e.g. chlorpromazine), tricyclic antidepressants (e.g. amitriptyline), opioids, alcohol**

Dosing:

oral:	epilepsy	900 to 1,800 mg/day in divided doses max 2,400 mg
	neuropathic pain	900 to 3,600 mg/day in divided doses
subcut:	not available	
rectal:	not available	

Syringe driver: not available

Mechanism of action: may act through effects on the synthesis of GABA in the CNS

Glycopyrrolate

Class: anticholinergic - antisecretory/antispasmodic

Indications (NB some may be unlicensed): antisecretory premedication, adjunctive peptic ulceration treatment, excess/retained secretions ('death rattle')

Contraindications/cautions: urinary retention, cardiac disease, glaucoma

Adverse reactions: *common* dry mouth, tachycardia; *less common* urinary retention, visual problems, dizziness, constipation, drowsiness

Metabolism/clearance: excreted in the bile and unchanged by the kidneys

Interactions:

- *additive anticholinergic effects* (e.g. dry mouth, urinary retention) with other drugs which have anticholinergic effects **e.g. cyclizine, amitriptyline, haloperidol, phenothiazines (e.g. chlorpromazine)**
- *decreased clinical effect (prokinetic effects)* of **metoclopramide/domperidone** may occur with concomitant glycopyrrolate

Dosing:

oral:	not available (not absorbed orally)
subcut:	200 to 600 micrograms/24 hours
rectal:	not available

Syringe driver: see compatibility chart

Mechanism of action: blocks cholinergic receptors

Initial response: (im): 30 to 45 minutes

Duration: (im): 7 hours

Notes:

- May be a useful alternative to hyoscine particularly in the elderly because it is less likely to cause CNS adverse effects as it does not readily cross the blood brain barrier.

Haloperidol

Class: antipsychotic - butyrophenone

Indications (NB some may be unlicensed): psychotic disorders, acute alcoholism, intractable nausea and vomiting, neuroleptanalgesia, hiccup

Contraindications/cautions: hepatic encephalopathy, epilepsy, Parkinson's disease, DLB

Adverse reactions: *common* extrapyramidal symptoms (usually at 5 to 20 mg/24 hours) e.g. oculogyric crisis, dystonia, tremor, abnormal movements, restlessness - may be less with parenteral route; *less common* hyperprolactinaemia, dry mouth, sedation, arrhythmias, QT prolongation

Metabolism/clearance: metabolised by metabolising enzyme CYP2D6 and 3A mainly in the liver

Interactions:

- *increased clinical effect/toxicity of haloperidol* (due to increased blood concentrations) may occur with some CYP metabolising enzyme inhibitors (see above) **e.g. aprepitant, bupropion, clarithromycin, fluoxetine, grapefruit juice, itraconazole, ketoconazole, paroxetine, valproate, voriconazole**
- *decreased clinical effect/toxicity of haloperidol* (due to decreased blood concentrations) may occur with some CYP metabolism enzyme inducers (see above) **e.g. carbamazepine, phenobarbitone, phenytoin, rifampicin, St John's wort**
- *increased clinical effect/toxicity of some drugs* (due to increased blood concentrations of them) may occur with haloperidol due to metabolising enzyme inhibition by haloperidol e.g. **amitriptyline, codeine** (decreased morphine concentrations so decreased clinical efficacy of codeine), **haloperidol, metoclopramide, nortriptyline, promethazine, tamoxifen** (decreased endoxifen (active metabolite) concentrations so decreased clinical effects)
- *additive CNS effects* with other CNS depressants **e.g. benzodiazepines (e.g. lorazepam), phenothiazines (e.g. chlorpromazine), tricyclic antidepressants (e.g. amitriptyline), opioids, alcohol**
- *enhanced extrapyramidal side effects* may occur with **lithium**
- *additive anticholinergic effects* (e.g. dry mouth, urinary retention) may occur with other drugs which have anticholinergic effects **e.g. cyclizine, amitriptyline, phenothiazines**

Dosing:

oral : parenteral = 3 : 2

nausea/vomiting		delirium (see notes)	
oral:	1.5 to 3 mg once a day	oral:	1.5 to 20 mg per 24 hours
subcut:	1 to 2 mg/24 hours	subcut:	1 to 15 mg/24 hours
		iv:	2 to 5 mg (at1mg/minute)

Syringe driver: see syringe driver compatibility table

Mechanism of action: nausea/vomiting - blocks dopamine receptors in the chemo-receptor trigger zone thus blocking input into the vomiting centre; delirium - may rebalance the unbalanced cholinergic/dopaminergic systems seen in delirium

continued

Peak effect: oral: 2 to 6 hours im/subcut: 20minutes

Duration: up to 24 hours

Notes:

- Useful as an antiemetic where causes of nausea and vomiting are biochemical imbalance or toxins.
- Particularly useful in opioid induced nausea and vomiting. It may be given as a single oral dose at night. Doses greater than 3 mg daily add no benefit.
- Delirium: The primary pharmacological intervention for delirium is to tranquillise (to control psychotic features). Occasionally sedation (to induce sleep) is an additional requirement. (See delirium page)

Hydromorphone*

Class: analgesic - opioid

Indication (NB some may be unlicensed): step 3 on the WHO ladder for severe pain, more effective in nociceptive than in neuropathic/visceral pains, severe breathlessness, cough, diarrhoea

Contraindications/cautions: hydromorphone hypersensitivity/allergy (this doesn't mean nausea/hallucination with opioids)

Adverse reactions: *common* nausea/vomiting in 10 to 30% of patients (usually transient for 1 to 5 days) - give haloperidol, constipation in 90% of patients - give a stimulant & softener laxative prophylactically, dry mouth, dizziness, sedation (usually transient and on initiation or dose increase); *less common* respiratory depression (high doses) - pain is an antidote - give naloxone if severe, visual problems - may see things upside down/flipping, myoclonic jerking - sign of toxicity - try a different opioid, delirium in 2% of patients - give haloperidol; rare hallucinations, hyperalgesia, raised intracranial pressure, biliary/urinary tract spasm, muscle rigidity, pruritus, pulmonary oedema, physical dependence (irrelevant in dying)

Metabolism/clearance: metabolised mainly in the liver by glucuronidation to active metabolites one of which is excreted by the kidneys so watch for accumulation in renal dysfunction

Interactions:

- *additive CNS effects* with other CNS depressants **e.g. benzodiazepines (e.g. lorazepam), phenothiazines (e.g. chlorpromazine), tricyclic antidepressants (e.g. amitriptyline), other opioids, MAO inhibitors**

Dosing:

pain

oral: initially 0.25 to 1 mg 4 hourly and prn

- prescribe rescue doses of 1/5th to 1/6th of the total 24 hour dose 4 to 6 hourly
- there is no real maximum dose but it is usually less than 200 mg/24 hours. If it is
- > 40 mg/24 hours consider the aetiology of the pain and the use of co-analgesia
- review doses regularly

subcut:	oral: subcut	=	2:1
rectal:	oral: rectal	=	1:1
epidural:	subcut:epidural	=	10:1
intrathecal	subcut:intrathecal	=	100:1

breathlessness, cough

oral: 0. 5 to 1 mg 4 hourly prn

Syringe driver: see syringe driver compatibility table

Mechanism of action: stimulates mu (and other) opioid receptors in the CNS and gastrointestinal tract

Peak effect: oral: 1 hour

Duration: oral: 4 to 5 hours

* **Drugs that are either not available or not funded in New Zealand**

continued

Notes:

- Tolerance to effect does occur but progressive disease is also a cause of dose fade.
- Toxicity: decrease in respiratory rate, mental status and blood pressure - give naloxone (see naloxone page).
- For conversion to morphine, oxycodone, fentanyl or methadone, see relevant pages.
- Hydromorphone can affect the ability to drive. Some patients may need to be told not to drive while taking hydromorphone. Always advise patients not to drive for several days after a dose increase.

Hyoscine butylbromide

Class: antispasmodic - gastrointestinal tract

Indications (NB some may be unlicensed): GI spasm/colic, some action as anti-emetic and antisecretory, sialorrhoea, 'death rattle'

Contraindications/cautions: megacolon, stenosis, glaucoma, tachycardia, urinary retention

Adverse reactions: *common* dry mouth; *less common* urinary retention, tachycardia, visual problems, dizziness, constipation

Metabolism/clearance: metabolised but also some excreted unchanged by the kidneys so care in renal dysfunction

Interactions:

- *additive anticholinergic effects* (e.g. dry mouth, urinary retention) may occur with other drugs which have anticholinergic effects **e.g. cyclizine, amitriptyline, phenothiazines (e.g. chlorpromazine)**
- *decreased clinical effect (prokinetic effects)* of **metoclopramide/domperidone** may occur with concomitant hyoscine butylbromide

Dosing:

oral:	20 mg 4 times a day
subcut:	40 to 100 mg/24 hours
rectal:	not available

Syringe driver: see syringe driver compatibility table

Mechanism of action: blocks the effect of acetylcholine on gastrointestinal smooth muscle causing relaxation

Onset: oral: 1 to 2 hours   subcut: 5 to 10 minutes

Duration: oral: 2 hours or less

Notes:

- May be useful with steroids in intestinal obstruction.
- Doesn't cross the blood-brain barrier so doesn't cause drowsiness or have a central antiemetic action.
- Only 8 to 10% absorbed orally.

Hyoscine hydrobromide

Class: anticholinergic - antisecretory

Indications (NB some may be unlicensed): premedication for sedation/amnesia, nausea/vomiting from motion sickness, 'death rattle'

Contraindications/cautions: elderly, urinary retention, cardiac disease, glaucoma

Adverse reactions: *common* dry mouth, tachycardia, hypotension (especially with morphine); *less common* urinary retention, visual problems, dizziness, constipation, drowsiness, hallucinations (commoner in the elderly)

Interactions:

- *additive anticholinergic effects* (e.g. dry mouth, urinary retention) may occur with other drugs which have anticholinergic effects **e.g. cyclizine, amitriptyline, phenothiazines (e.g. chlorpromazine)**
- *decreased clinical effect (prokinetic effects)* of **metoclopramide/domperidone** may occur with concomitant hyoscine

Dosing:

oral: not available
subcut (as the hydrobromide): 0.4 to 2.4 mg/24 hours (usually 0.8 to 1.2 mg stat)
rectal: not available
patch: 1 patch (1.5 mg)/72 hours (behind the ear)

Syringe driver: see syringe driver compatibility table

Mechanism of action: blocks cholinergic receptors in CNS and the gastrointestinal tract

Peak response: im: 1 to 2 hours (antisecretory)

Duration: im: 8 hours

Notes:

- Thought to cross the blood brain barrier more easily then hyoscine butylbromide.
- Risk of confusion in the elderly is high.
- May be particularly useful in nausea and vomiting related to motion.

Ketamine

Class: anaesthetic

Indications (NB some may be unlicensed): general anaesthesia (400-700 mg im), severe pain (at sub-anaesthetic doses), opioid tolerance reversal, neuropathic pain

Contraindications/cautions: hypertension, tendency to hallucinations, alcohol abuse, epilepsy

Adverse reactions: *common* hallucinations (see notes below), delirium, tachycardia, hypertension; *less common* hypotension, bradycardia laryngospasm, diplopia, respiratory depression

Metabolism/clearance: may be metabolised in the liver by CYP metabolising enzymes. Active metabolite - norketamine

Interactions:

- *additive CNS effects* with other CNS depressants **e.g. benzodiazepines (e.g. lorazepam), phenothiazines (e.g. chlorpromazine), tricyclic antidepressants (e.g. amitriptyline), opioids, alcohol**

Dosing:

oral:	injection has been given orally, capsules and lozenges are available as below
subcut:	100 to 500 mg in 24 hours as a 'pulse' over 5 days. Give a test dose of 10 mg before starting infusion.
rectal:	not available

Syringe driver: see syringe driver compatibility table

Mechanism of action: in pain thought to act at NMDA receptors in the dorsal horn

Peak effect: iv: 10 to 15 minutes

Duration: iv: 15 to 30minutes

Notes:

- May be useful in opioid tolerance/intolerance, in 'wind-up' (or rapidly escalating doses) and may allow a reduction in opioid dose.
- May be useful in neuropathic pain although 'pulse' therapy has been shown to be no better than placebo in one study.
- If hallucinations occur reduce the dose of ketamine and give a benzodiazepine (e.g. diazepam 5 mg orally, midazolam 5 mg subcutaneously) or haloperidol 2 to 5 mg orally or subcutaneously.
- Has been effective when used topically.
- 'Pulse' therapy (increasing subcutaneous doses over 3 to 5 days) may be sufficient to 'reset' the NMDA/opioid receptors. Give 100 mg/24 hours then 200 mg/24hrs then 300 mg/24hrs for 3 days then consider discontinuation.
- Oral administration usually involves lower doses e.g. 25 to 50 mg 3 times a day as more norketamine is produced due to first pass metabolism. Norketamine is active and may be more potent than the parent ketamine.
- Oral formulations include the injection given orally either straight or made up into a syrup (see www.palliativedrugs.com for formula), oral lozenges and oral capsules.
- Sublingual use of the injection may also be effective.
- May have a role treating severe depressive disorders.

Levetiracetam

Class: anticonvulsant

Indications: seizure control

Contraindications/cautions: monitor for behavioural changes, hepatic and renal impairment

Adverse reactions: *common* somnolence, asthenia, infection, GI disturbance, blurred vision, hostility, pruritis

Metabolism/clearance: metabolised by hydrolysis. Fraction excreted unchanged in the urine is 0.7

Interactions:

- *increased clinical effect/toxicity of levetiracetam* may occur with other drugs that are excreted by active tubular secretion **e.g. probenecid**
- *increased clinical effect/toxicity of levetiracetam* (due to increased blood concentrations) may occur with **valproate**
- *decreased clinical effect/toxicity of levetiracetam* (due to decreased blood concentrations) may occur with **carbamazepine, phenobarbitone, phenytoin**

Dosing:

oral:	500 mg twice daily initially (reduce in renal impairment)
subcut:	not available
rectal:	not available

Syringe driver: not available

Mechanism of action: inhibits Ca2+ currents and reduces the release of Ca2+ from intraneuronal stores. Reverses the reductions in GABA- and glycine-gated currents induced by zinc and β-carbolines.

Onset: peak concentrations at 1.5 hours

Levomepromazine (Methotrimeprazine)

Class: antipsychotic/neuroleptic - phenothiazine

Indications (NB some may be unlicensed): psychosis, severe 'terminal' pain with anxiety/distress/restlessness, schizophrenia, with other analgesics for pain, anxiety and distress, nausea/vomiting

Contraindications/cautions: hepatic dysfunction, encephalopathy, Parkinson's disease, DLB

Adverse reactions: *common* somnolence, postural hypotension, sedation; *less common* dry mouth, hypotension, extrapyramidal side effects (long term high dose usually)

Metabolism/clearance: metabolised by sulphonation then glucuronidation. Metabolites may be active and are excreted by the kidneys so care in renal dysfunction. May inhibit CYP2D6.

Interactions:

- *increased clinical effect/toxicity of some drugs* (due to increased blood concentrations of them) may occur with levomepromazine (methotrimeprazine) due to metabolising enzyme inhibition by levomepromazine (methotrimeprazine) **e.g. amitriptyline, codeine** (decreased morphine concentrations so decreased clinical efficacy of codeine), **fluoxetine, nortriptyline, oxycodone, paroxetine, promethazine**
- *additive CNS effects* with other CNS depressants **e.g. benzodiazepines (e.g. lorazepam), other phenothiazines (e.g. chlorpromazine), tricyclic antidepressants (e.g. amitriptyline), opioids, alcohol**
- *additive increased risk of QT interval prolongation* (cardiac adverse effect which may lead to arrhythmias) with **tricyclic antidepressants (e.g. amitriptyline), flecainide, erythromycin, theophylline, domperidone**

Dosing:

	pain, restlessness, distress, delirium	*nausea/vomiting*
oral:	6.25 to 50 mg every 4 to 8 hours	6.25 to 12.5 mg daily
subcut:	6.25 to 200 mg/24 hours	6.25 to 12.5 mg/24 hours
rectal:	not available	

Syringe driver: dilute with 0.9% sodium chloride - see syringe driver compatibility table

Mechanism of action: suppresses sensory impulses in the CNS via various neuro-transmitters.

Onset: im/?subcut (analgesia): 20 to 40 minutes

Duration: im/?subcut: 12 to 24 hours   Half life: 15 to 30 hours

Notes:

- Only phenothiazine with analgesic properties.
- Doses of less than 25 mg/24 hours are associated with minimal sedation.
- Benztropine 2 mg may be useful in alleviating extrapyramidal side effects.
- May be a useful option in patients with multiple symptoms.
- For smaller doses disperse tablets in water and give a fraction of it.

Loperamide

Class: antidiarrhoeal - peripheral opioid receptor agonist

Indications: diarrhoea, reduce number of stools in ileostomy and colostomy patients

Contraindications/cautions: diarrhoea due to infection or antibiotics

Adverse reactions: *common* flatulence, constipation, abdominal distension, abdominal pain, bloating; *less common* giddiness, dry mouth

Metabolism/clearance: transported out of cells by P-glycoprotein which stops it crossing the blood-brain barrier. Metabolised by oxidation but 50% excreted unchanged in faeces.

Interactions:

- *decreased clinical effect of loperamide* with *prokinetics* **e.g. metoclopramide/ domperidone**
- *CNS adverse effects may occur with* P-glycoprotein inhibitors **e.g. grapefruit juice, itraconazole, ketoconazole, tamoxifen**

Dosing:

oral:	2 mg after each loose stool (max. of 16 mg/24 hours)
subcut:	not available
rectal:	not available

Syringe driver: not available

Mechanism of action: binds to opioid receptors in gastrointestinal tract. May also affect cholinergic receptors.

Onset: 1 to 3 hours

Notes:

- May not be of benefit if patient is already taking morphine.
- Absorbed but doesn't normally cross the blood-brain barrier BUT may become active in the CNS as an opioid if given with P-glycoprotein inhibitors e.g. itraconazole.

Lorazepam

Class: anxiolytic - short acting benzodiazepine

Indications (NB some may be unlicensed): anxiety, insomnia, premedication, muscle spasm, nausea/vomiting (anxiety related)

Contraindications/cautions: respiratory failure

Adverse reactions: *common* sedation, dizziness, unsteadiness; *less common* respiratory depression (high dose), disorientation, depression, disinhibition, amnesia, excitement

Metabolism/clearance: Mainly metabolised by glucuronidation

Interactions:

- *additive CNS effects* with other CNS depressants **e.g. other benzodiazepines (e.g. midazolam), phenothiazines (e.g. chlorpromazine), tricyclic antidepressants (e.g. amitriptyline), opioids, alcohol**

Dosing:

oral:	anxiety 1 to 3 mg/day in 2 to 3 doses (max. 10 mg/24 hours)	insomnia 1 to 2 mg at bedtime
subcut:	injection available (unregistered) but difficult to obtain	
rectal:	not available	

Syringe driver: not available

Mechanism of action: may enhance the effect of GABA, an inhibitory neurotransmitter in the CNS

Onset: oral: 20 to 30 minutes sublingual: shorter onset

Duration: oral: 6 to 8 hours Half life: 10 to 20 hours

Notes:

- Lorazepam is a short acting benzodiazepine.
- Tablets may be tried sublingually.
- Not metabolised by metabolising enzymes CYP450 so less likely to interact with other drugs compared with other benzodiazepines.
- Theoretically most appropriate benzodiazepine to use in hepatic failure.
- For approximate equivalent oral anxiolytic/sedative doses see clonazepam page.
- For pharmacological properties of benzodiazepines see clonazepam page.

Methadone

Class: analgesic - opioid

Indications (NB some may be unlicensed): step 3 in the WHO analgesic ladder, cough, opioid dependence

Contraindications/cautions: may accumulate as long half life

Adverse reactions: *see morphine* but less drowsiness, nausea and constipation. Has a long and variable half life so watch for signs of accumulation e.g. decreased respiratory rate or mental status (particularly in the elderly).

Metabolism/clearance: metabolised by metabolising enzyme CYP3A mainly in the liver. Demethylation is the major route of metabolism and metabolites are excreted by the kidney.

Interactions:

- *increased clinical effect/toxicity of methadone* (due to increased blood concentrations) may occur with some CYP metabolising enzyme inhibitors (see above) **e.g. aprepitant, clarithromycin, grapefruit juice, indinavir, itraconazole, ketoconazole, nelfinavir, ritonavir, telapravir, voriconazole**
- *decreased clinical effect/toxicity of methadone* (due to decreased blood concentrations) may occur with some CYP metabolising enzyme inducers (see above) **e.g. carbamazepine, phenobarbitone, phenytoin, rifampicin, St John's wort**
- *additive CNS effects* (including respiratory depression) with other **CNS depressants e.g. benzodiazepines (e.g. lorazepam), phenothiazines (e.g. chlorpromazine), tricyclic antidepressants (e.g. amitriptyline), other opioids, alcohol**
- *additive increased risk of QT interval prolongation* (cardiac adverse effect which may lead to arrhythmias) with other drugs that prolong it.

Dosing: (and see notes)

oral:	2.5 to 5 mg twice daily initially
subcut:	50 to 75% of oral dose
rectal:	not available in NZ

Syringe driver: see syringe driver compatibility table

Mechanism of action: stimulates opioid receptors in the CNS and gastrointestinal tract and also thought to act at the NMDA receptor

Onset: 0.5 to 1 hour initially

Duration: 6 to 8 hours initially then 22 to 48 hours on repeat dosing

Notes:

- May be useful in opioid rotation.
- Dose conversion ratios from other opioids is variable as individuals have differing methadone half lives and the ratio varies with dose (see next page).
- As affects NMDA receptors may prevent 'wind up' (rapidly escalating doses) on long term use and is useful in neuropathic pain.
- Renal and hepatic impairment are rarely a problem.
- Subcutaneous injection/infusion may be irritant.
- Some centres use low dose methadone alongside other opioids.
- In opioid naïve patients starting doses are usually 2.5 to 5 mg twice a day with 3 hourly prn breakthrough doses. Titrate dose weekly.

Conversion to methadone

Toombs/Ayonide method

- Convert total daily dose of morphine (or equivalent) to equivalent predicted total daily dose of methadone using the nomogram below
- Divide the predicted total daily dose of methadone by 3 and give this dose 8 hourly e.g. total daily dose of 300 mg oral morphine (or equivalent) = total daily oral dose of methadone of 30 mg i.e. 10 mg 8 hourly.
- Breakthrough - methadone 1/10th the total daily methadone 2 hourly i.e. 10 mg 8 hourly breakthrough dose of 3 mg or continue with the original opioid for breakthrough

Based on ratios by Ayonide, 2000:

mg oral morphine	ratio of morphine:methadone
<100	3:1
101-300	5:1
301-600	10:1
601-800	12:1
801-1000	15:1
>1001	20:1

Methadone Conversion Nomogram – Predicted Dose

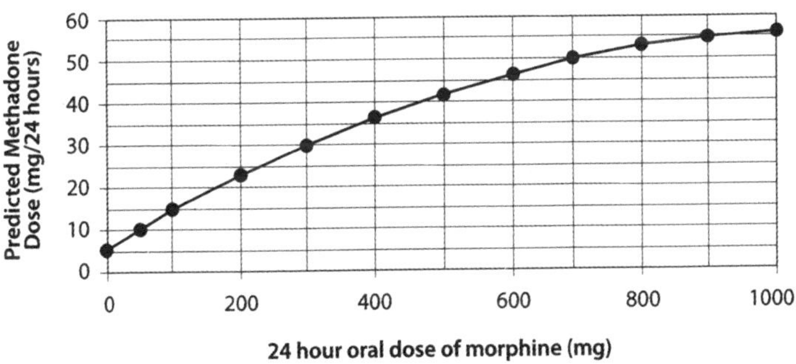

Toombs J Oral methadone dosing for chronic pain. A practioner's guide. 2008 Pain Treatment Topics,
Ayonide OT et al The rediscovery of methadone for cancer pain management. Med J Aust. 2000 173:536-540

Methylphenidate

Class: central stimulant - amphetamine related

Indications (NB some may be unlicensed): attention deficit hyperactivity disorder (possible restrictions), narcolepsy, depression, neurobehavioural symptoms in brain tumours/injuries

Contraindications/cautions: anxiety, glaucoma, agitation, hyperthyroidism, cardiac problems, hypertension, epilepsy

Adverse reactions: *common* nervousness, insomnia, tachycardia, urticarial; *less common* blurred vision, hallucinations, blood disorders, psychosis (very high doses), arrhythmias

Metabolism/clearance: metabolised by hydrolysis. Inactive metabolite is excreted by the kidneys.

Interactions:

- *increased analgesia and decreased sedation* may occur with some **opioids**
- *hypertensive crisis may occur with concomitant* **MAOIs (e.g. tranylcypromine)**
- *decreased hypotensive effect* of **adrenergic blockers (e.g. terazosin) may occur with concomitant methylphenidate**
- *hypertension with* **tricyclic antidepressants (e.g. amitriptyline)** may occur

Dosing:

depression (max. adult dose of 1 mg/kg/24 hours)

oral:	normal release	10 to 30 mg a day (morning and mid-day)
subcut:	not available	
rectal:	not available	

Syringe driver: not available

Mechanism of action: acts as a stimulant in the CNS

Onset: depression: 2 to 5 days

Notes:

- Patients may respond to short courses of 2 to 3 weeks then withdraw.
- Methylphenidate is occasionally used to treat opioid-induced drowsiness.

Metoclopramide

Class: antiemetic - prokinetic

Indications: nausea and/or vomiting, restoration of tone in upper GI tract, hiccups

Contraindications/cautions: complete intestinal obstruction. Young persons (< 20 years old) are more prone to extrapyramidal side effects so use lower doses

Adverse reactions: *less common* tardive dyskinesia - usually on prolonged use, extrapyramidal reactions e.g. Parkinsonism, akathisia (usually at doses > 30 mg/24 hours - switch to domperidone which enters the CNS to a lesser extent), diarrhoea, restlessness

Metabolism/clearance: metabolised in the liver partially by the metabolising enzyme CYP2D6 to inactive metabolites which are mainly excreted with some parent drug by the kidneys

Interactions:

- *increased clinical effect/toxicity of metoclopramide* (due to increased blood concentrations) may occur with some CYP metabolising enzyme inhibitors (see above) **e.g. bupropion, fluoxetine, paroxetine, quinine**
- *faster onset of action of* **SR morphine** may occur with concomitant metoclopramide
- *prokinetic activity of metoclopramide* may be affected by concomitant **opioids, anticholinergics e.g. hyoscine**
- *increased risk of extrapyramidal effects and neurotoxicity with* **lithium**

Dosing:

oral:	10 mg 3 times a day (max. 0.5 mg/kg)
subcut:	30 to 60 mg over 24 hours (watch for extrapyramidal effects at > 30 mg/24 hours)
rectal:	10 mg up to 3 times a day

Syringe driver: see syringe driver compatibility table

Mechanism of action: blocks dopamine receptors and perhaps affects 5HT receptors in the gastro-intestinal tract (increasing peristalsis), CNS and chemoreceptor-trigger zone (CTZ)

Peak effect: oral/rectal: 1 to 3 hours

Notes:

- 'High dose' metoclopramide may work via 5HT3 antagonism (like ondansetron) but is associated with severe extrapyramidal effects.
- Most effective for nausea/vomiting due to gastric stasis. Some clinicians believe that metoclopramide is no better than placebo as an antiemetic but is useful as a prokinetic.
- Benztropine 2 mg may be used as an antidote.
- The European Medicines Agency's Committee recommends that metoclopramide should only be prescribed for short-term use (up to five days) and that it should only be used as a second-line.

Metronidazole

Class: antibiotic - anti-anaerobe

Indications (NB some may be unlicensed): bacterial infections, useful in controlling malodorous wounds

Adverse reactions: *common* GI upset, urticaria, metallic taste, furry tongue; *less common* drowsiness, headache, dizziness, urine darkening, blood disorders, muscle/ joint pain

Metabolism/clearance: metabolised in the liver to some active and some inactive metabolites which are excreted with some parent drug by the kidneys

Interactions:

- *disulfiram-like reaction* (nausea, vomiting, sweating) may occur with concomitant alcohol
- *increased toxicity of* **lithium** may occur with metronidazole

Dosing:

oral:	800 mg stat then 400 mg 3 times a day
subcut:	injection available but not usually used subcut
iv:	500mg 3 times a day (infusion)
rectal:	1 g 3 times a day for 3 days then twice a day
topical:	apply twice a day

Syringe driver: not applicable

Mechanism of action: in malodorous wounds kills anaerobes responsible for the smell

*** Drugs that are either not available or not funded in New Zealand**

Miconazole

Class: antifungal - imidazole

Indications: fungal infection - topical, oral, GI, vaginal

Contraindications/cautions: hepatic impairment

Adverse reactions: *common* oral gel - GI upset; *less common* oral gel - hepatitis, topical/vaginal- burning, itching

Metabolism/clearance: metabolised by the liver

Interactions: Oral gel/vaginal preparations (absorption is likely)

- *decreased clinical effect* of **amphotericin** may occur with miconazole
- *may affect INR* of patients taking **warfarin**. Monitor even if only using oral gel.

Dosing:

mouth (topical):50 mg 4 times a day for 7 days

subcut: not available

rectal: not available

topical: apply twice a day

vaginal: use at night

Syringe driver: not available

Mechanism of action: increases fungal cell membrane permeability

Microlax™/Micolette™

(Sodium citrate 450 mg, sodium lauryl sulphoacetate 45 mg, sorbitol 3.125 g, sorbic acid 5 mg, water to 5 mL)

Class: rectal laxative - stimulant, faecal softener and osmotic

Indications: constipation, bowel evacuation

Dosing:

oral:	not available
subcut:	not available
rectal:	1 tube as required

Syringe driver: not available

Mechanism of action: may stimulate colonic activity via nerves in the intestinal mucosa (sodium citrate) and increased fluid uptake by stools thus softening them (sodium lauryl sulphoacetate, sorbitol)

Onset: almost immediate

Midazolam

Class: sedative - benzodiazepine

Indications (NB some may be unlicensed): sedation, anaesthetic induction agent, hiccups, epilepsy, muscle spasm, dyspnoea, insomnia

Contraindications/cautions: avoid sudden withdrawal, respiratory depression

Adverse reactions: *common* fatigue, drowsiness, amnesia; *less common* respiratory depression (high dose), aggression, confusion, hypotension

Metabolism/clearance: metabolised by metabolising enzyme CYP3A (major) mainly in the liver

Interactions:

- *increased clinical effect/toxicity of midazolam* (due to increased blood concentrations) may occur with some CYP metabolising enzyme inhibitors (see above) **e.g. clarithromycin, fluconazole, grapefruit juice, itraconazole, ketoconazole**
- *decreased clinical effect/toxicity of midazolam* (due to decreased blood concentrations) may occur with some CYP metabolism enzyme inducers (see above) **e.g. carbamazepine, phenobarbitone, phenytoin, rifampicin, St John's wort**
- *additive CNS effects* with other CNS depressants **e.g. other benzodiazepines (e.g. lorazepam), phenothiazines (e.g. chlorpromazine), tricyclic antidepressants (e.g. amitriptyline), opioids, alcohol**

Dosing:

oral:	7.5 to 15 mg at bed-time
subcut.	5 to 60 mg/24 hours (up to 150 mg in sedation at the end-of-life)
rectal:	not available

Syringe driver: see syringe driver compatibility table

Mechanism of action: may enhance the effect of GABA, an inhibitory neurotransmitter in the CNS

Peak concentrations:

oral: 20 to 50 min subcut: 5 to 10 min iv: 2 to 3 mins

Duration: 15 minutes to several hours

Half life: 2 to 5 hours

Notes:

- Midazolam is a very short acting benzodiazepine so dose titration to response is easier than with longer acting benzodiazepines e.g. clonazepam.
- iv administration can result in hypotension and transient apnoea.
- Benzodiazepines may reduce dyspnoea by anxiolytic and sedative effects.
- For approximate equivalent oral anxiolytic/sedative doses see clonazepam page.
- For pharmacological properties of benzodiazepines and other hypnotics see clonazepam page.
- May be used bucally.

Mirtazapine

Class: antidepressant – central presynaptic alpha 2 and 5HT antagonist

Indications (NB some may be unlicensed): major depression, nausea

Contraindications/cautions: bipolar depression, epilepsy, cardiac disease, prostatic hypertrophy, diabetes, abrupt withdrawal

Adverse reactions: *common* increased appetite, dizziness, headache, dry mouth; *less common* convulsions, tremor, nightmares, mania, syncope, hyponatraemia, nausea

Metabolism/clearance: metabolised by metabolising enzyme CYP2D6, 1A2 and 3A mainly in the liver to at least one active metabolite (by CYP3A)

Interactions:

- *increased clinical effect/toxicity of mirtazapine* (due to increased blood concentrations of parent) may occur with some CYP metabolising enzyme inhibitors (see above) **e.g. bupropion, aprepitant, ciprofloxacin, clarithromycin, fluconazole, fluoxetine, grapefruit juice, itraconazole, ketoconazole, paroxetine, quinine**
- *decreased clinical effect/toxicity of mirtazapine* (due to decreased blood concentrations of parent) may occur with some CYP metabolism enzyme inducers (see above) **e.g. broccoli, carbamazepine, dexamethasone, phenobarbitone, phenytoin, prednisone, rifampicin, smoking, St John's wort**
- *additive risk of serotonin syndrome* (potentially fatal syndrome - symptoms include sweating, diarrhoea, confusion) with other serotonergic drugs **e.g. amitriptyline, carbamazepine, fluoxetine, paroxetine, tramadol, lithium**

Dosing:

oral:	15 to 45 mg at bed-time
subcut:	not available

Syringe driver: not available

Mechanism of action: blocks presynaptic alpha 2 and 5HT2 and 3 receptors increasing central noradrenaline and serotonin (blocking 5HT2 and 5HT3 receptors allowing stimulation of 5HT1 receptors)

Peak concentrations: oral: 2 hours

Half life: 20 to 40 hours

Morphine

Class: analgesic - opioid

Indications (NB some may be unlicensed): step 3 on the WHO ladder for severe pain, more effective in nociceptive than in neuropathic/visceral pains, severe breathlessness, cough, diarrhoea

Contraindications/cautions: morphine hypersensitivity/allergy (not nausea/hallucination with opioids)

Adverse reactions: *common* nausea/vomiting in 10 to 30% of patients (usually transient for 1 to 5 days) - give haloperidol, constipation in 90% of patients - give a stimulant & softener laxative prophylactically, dry mouth, dizziness, sedation (usually transient and on initiation or dose increase); *less common* respiratory depression (high doses) - pain is an antidote - give naloxone if severe, visual problems - may see things upside down/flipping, myoclonic jerking - sign of toxicity - try a different opioid, delirium in 2% of patients - give haloperidol rare hallucinations, hyperalgesia, raised intracranial pressure, biliary/urinary tract spasm, muscle rigidity, pruritus, pulmonary oedema, physical dependence (irrelevant in dying)

Metabolism/clearance: metabolised mainly in the liver by glucuronidation to active metabolites one of which is excreted by the kidneys so watch for accumulation in renal dysfunction

Interactions:

- *additive CNS effects with other CNS depressants* **e.g. benzodiazepines (e.g. lorazepam), phenothiazines (e.g. chlorpromazine), tricyclic antidepressants (e.g. amitriptyline), other opioids**
- *faster onset of* action of **slow release morphine** may occur with **metoclopramide**

Dosing:

pain (initially use the normal release and titrate to pain)

oral:	normal release	initially 5 to 10 mg 4 hourly and prn
	slow release	initially 10 to 30 mg 12 hourly

- prescribe rescue doses (normal release) of 1/5th to 1/6th of the total 24 hour dose 4 to 6 hourly
- there is no real maximum dose but it is usually less than 200 mg/24 hours. If it is
- >400 mg/24 hours consider the aetiology of the pain and the use of co-analgesia or opioid rotation
- review doses regularly

subcut:	oral: subcut	=	2:1
rectal:	oral: rectal	=	1:1
epidural:	subcut:epidural	=	10:1
intrathecal	subcut:intrathecal	=	100:1

breathlessness, cough

oral: normal release 5 to 10 mg 4 hourly prn

Syringe driver: see syringe driver compatibility table

Mechanism of action: stimulates mu (and other) opioid receptors in the CNS and gastrointestinal tract

continued

Peak effect:	oral:	normal release	1 hour
Duration:	oral:	normal release	4 to 5 hours
	oral:	slow release	8 to 12 hours

Notes:

- Tolerance to effect does occur but progressive disease is also a cause of dose fade.
- If dose of slow release morphine is increased remember to also increase the prescribed dose of normal release morphine for breakthrough pain/rescue.
- Toxicity: decrease in respiratory rate, mental status and blood pressure - give naloxone (see naloxone page).
- For conversion to oxycodone, hydromorphone*, fentanyl or methadone, see relevant pages.
- Morphine can affect the ability to drive. Some patients may need to be told not to drive while taking morphine. Always advise patients not to drive for several days after a dose increase.
- Topical morphine may be useful for wound pain. It is usually used as 0.05 to 0.1% morphine [i.e. 0.5 to 1 mg/mL] in Intrasite™ gel, metronidazole gel or KY Jelly™.

*** Drugs that are either not available or not funded in New Zealand**

Movicol™, Lax-sachets™

(Macrogol 3350, sodium chloride, sodium bicarbonate, potassium chloride, potassium acesulfame)

Class: laxative - osmotic

Indications: constipation including faecal impaction

Contraindications/cautions: intestinal obstruction or perforation, ileus and severe inflammatory conditions, cardiac disease (contains sodium and potassium)

Adverse reactions: *less common* abdominal distension and pain, nausea

Metabolism/clearance: not absorbed

Interactions: few as not absorbed - may affect the absorption of some drugs

Dosing:

Movicol™, Lax-sachet™:

constipation	1 to 3 sachets per day
faecal impaction	8 sachets per day taken within 6 hours for a max. of 3 days. If cardiovascular problems, do not take more than 2 sachets over any 1 hour.

Each sachet should be dissolved in 125 mL. For faecal impaction dissolve 8 sachets in 1 L of water.

Movicol-Half™:

constipation	1 to 6 sachets/day
faecal impaction	16 sachets/day taken within 6 hours for a max. of 3 days. If cardiovascular problems, do not take more than 4 sachets over any 1 hour.

Each sachet should be dissolved in 60 mL of water.

Mechanism of action: osmotic action in the gut to increase liquid content of stools but with no net loss of sodium, potassium or water

Onset: faecal impaction: most cleared after 3 days

Notes:

- Effective laxative in palliative care.
- More acceptable to many than lactulose.

Naloxone

Class: opioid antagonist

Indications: opioid overdose

Unlicensed indications: may enhance opioid analgesia at very low dose, may attenuate opioid adverse effects e.g. nausea and vomiting at low dose

Contraindications/cautions: cardiovascular disease

Adverse reactions: *common* nausea, vomiting, tachycardia, sweating, raised blood pressure (opioid withdrawal)

Metabolism/clearance: metabolised mainly in the liver by glucuronidation

Interactions:

- *blocks the actions* of opioids e.g. morphine, fentanyl, methadone, oxycodone, hydromorphone*

Dosing:

If respiratory rate < 8 per minute, patient unconscious or cyanosed

iv:	0.1 to 0.2 mg every 2 to 3 minutes for reversal of CNS depression post-op
	0.4 to 2 mg every 2 to 3 minutes up to 10 mg for opioid overdose
oral:	not available alone
subcut:	see below
rectal:	not available

Syringe driver: not applicable

Mechanism of action: blocks action of opioids at opioid receptors

Onset: iv: 2 to 3 minutes subcut/im: 15 minutes

Duration: 15 to 90 minutes

Notes:

- Best given iv, however if not practical can be given im or subcut.
- Reversal of respiratory depression will result in reversal of analgesia and withdrawal symptoms if physiologically dependent.

*** Drugs that are either not available or not funded in New Zealand**

Naproxen

Class: non-steroidal anti-inflammatory drug (NSAID)

Indications (NB some may be unlicensed): pain associated with inflammation (including bone pain), dysmenorrhoea, itch, sweating

Contraindications/cautions: GI ulceration, asthma (in sensitive patients), renal, cardiac or hepatic impairment

Adverse reactions: *common* GI ulceration (more common if elderly, on steroids or aspirin), diarrhoea, indigestion, nausea; *less common* dizziness, rash, nephrotoxicity, hepatitis, oedema, hypertension, headache, tinnitus, proctitis (rectal administration). NB Inhibits platelet aggregation - may prolong bleeding time.

Metabolism/clearance: metabolised by metabolising enzyme CYP2C8/9 mainly in the liver

Interactions:

- *increased clinical effect/toxicity of naproxen* (due to increased blood concentrations) may occur with some CYP metabolising enzyme inhibitors (see above) **e.g. fluconazole, ketoconazole, voriconazole**
- *decreased clinical effect/toxicity of naproxen* (due to decreased blood concentrations) may occur with some CYP metabolism enzyme inducers (see above) **e.g. phenobarbitone, phenytoin, rifampicin**
- *increased clinical effect/toxicity of* **lithium, digoxin, methotrexate** and **warfarin** may occur with naproxen due to increased concentrations of these drugs via kidney excretion competition so monitor
- *decreased clinical effects of* **diuretics (e.g. frusemide)** and **beta blockers (e.g. propranolol)** may occur with naproxen
- *increased risk of renal toxicity and hyperkalaemia* with **ACE inhibitors (e.g. enalapril)** may occur with naproxen
- *additive risk of bleeding* may occur with **warfarin** and **heparin** in combination with naproxen

Dosing:

oral:	normal release	500 to 1,000 mg per day in 2 divided doses or 275 mg every 6 to 8 hours (max 1,375 mg)
	sustained release	750 to 1,000 mg per day as a single dose
subcut:		not available
rectal:		not available (try diclofenac)

Syringe driver: not available

Mechanism of action: inhibits prostaglandin synthesis which are involved in inflammation and pain

Peak effect: oral (normal release): 2 to 4 hours

Duration: 7 hours

Nortriptyline

Class: antidepressant - tricyclic

Indications (NB some may be unlicensed): depression, smoking cessation, neuropathic pain, itch

Contraindications/cautions: arrhythmias, recent MI, epilepsy (lowers seizure threshold), urinary retention

Adverse reactions: *common* anticholinergic - dry mouth, blurred vision, urinary retention, drowsiness (tolerance to these may develop except dry mouth); *less common* sweating, constipation, confusion, arrhythmias, tachycardia, postural hypotension.

Metabolism/clearance: metabolised by the metabolising enzyme CYP2D6 (major) mainly in the liver to active metabolites

Interactions:

- *increased clinical effect/toxicity of nortriptyline* (due to increased blood concentrations) may occur with some CYP metabolising enzyme inhibitors (see above) **e.g. bupropion, fluoxetine, paroxetine, quinine**
- *additive risk of serotonin syndrome* (potentially fatal syndrome - symptoms include sweating, diarrhoea, confusion) with other serotonergic drugs **e.g. carbamazepine, fluoxetine**
- *additive drowsiness may* occur with alcohol, **benzodiazepines (e.g. clonazepam)**
- *increased risk of seizures in epileptics* may occur with nortriptyline so interacts with anticonvulsants **e.g. phenytoin**
- *additive CNS effects* with other **CNS depressants e.g. benzodiazepines (e.g. lorazepam), phenothiazines (e.g. chlorpromazine), opioids, alcohol**
- *additive increased risk of QT interval prolongation* (cardiac adverse effect which may lead to arrhythmias) with other drugs that prolong the QT interval **e.g. lignocaine, lithium, haloperidol**

Dosing:

	depression	*pain*
oral:	25 to 100 mg at night (max. of 50 mg in elderly)	10 to 50 mg at night
subcut:	not available	
rectal:	not available	

Syringe driver: not available

Mechanism of action: not really understood but thought to be through noradrenaline and serotonin in the CNS

Onset: depression: 2 to 6 weeks pain: several days

Notes:

- Metabolite of amitriptyline, less adverse reactions (including sedation) than amitriptyline.
- 25 mg nortriptyline ≈ 75 mg amitriptyline (approx).
- Measurement of blood drug concentrations may be useful to establish compliance or confirm toxicity.

Nystatin

Class: antifungal - polyene

Indications: fungal infections - topical, oral, gastrointestinal, vaginal

Adverse reactions: *less common* nausea, vomiting, diarrhoea (at high doses), local irritation

Dosing:

oral: (not absorbed orally)	
oral candidiasis:	100,000 units (1 mL) 4 times a day
gastrointestinal candidiasis:	500,000 to 1,000,000 units 3 times a day
subcut:	not available
rectal:	not available
topical:	apply 2 to 3 times a day
vaginal:	5 g of cream once or twice a day

Syringe driver: not available

Mechanism of action: increases fungal cell membrane permeability

Notes:

- If infection is severe or recurrent use a systemic antifungal e.g. fluconazole.

Octreotide

Class: growth hormone inhibitor

Indications (NB some may be unlicensed): acromegaly, gastro-entero pancreatic endocrine tumours, post pancreatic surgery, emergency treatment to stop bleeding oesophageal varices, antisecretory in intestinal obstruction, secretory diarrhoea, high fistula output, variceal bleeds

Contraindications/cautions: diabetes

Adverse reactions: *less common* injection site reaction, gastro upset, hepatitis, gallstones, hyper/hypoglycaemia, bradycardia, dizziness, drowsiness, headache, hypothyroidism

Metabolism/clearance: metabolised by the liver

Interactions:

- *decreased absorption of* **ciclosporin** may occur with octreotide

Dosing:

oral:	not available
subcut:	200 to 600 micrograms/24 hours (max. 1 mg/24 hours) LAR - not usually used in palliative care
rectal:	not available
iv:	not available

Syringe driver: see syringe driver compatibility table

Mechanism of action: blocks somatostatin receptors

Peak effect: 30 minutes

Duration: 12 hours

Notes:

- Long acting octreotide formulations are available. Their use in palliative care has not been fully established.

Olanzapine

Class: antipsychotic, antimanic, mood stabiliser

Indications (NB some may be unlicensed): acute and chronic psychoses including schizophrenia, bipolar disorder, nausea and vomiting, delirium

Contraindications/cautions: liver dysfunction, cardiovascular and cerebrovascular disease, hypotension, seizures, blood disorders, renal dysfunction, prostatic hypertrophy, paralytic ileus, bone marrow depression, diabetes, narrow angle glaucoma, hypercholesteraemia, Parkinson's disease, DLB

Adverse reactions: *common* drowsiness, weight gain, dizziness, hallucinations, akathisia and other extrapyramidal side effects, elevated blood glucose and triglycerides, chest pain, oedema, constipation, dry mouth; *less common* angioedema, urticaria, diabetic coma, hepatitis, pancreatitis, priapism, tardive dyskinesia, neuroleptic malignant syndrome, blood disorders, hypotension, mania, seizures

Metabolism/clearance: metabolised mainly in the liver by the metabolising enzymes CYP1A2 to inactive metabolites which are partially excreted by the kidneys

Interactions:

- *increased clinical effect/toxicity of olanzapine* (due to increased blood concentrations) may occur with some CYP metabolising enzyme inhibitors (see above) **e.g. ciprofloxacin, ketoconazole**
- *decreased clinical effect/toxicity of olanzapine* (due to decreased blood concentrations) may occur with some CYP metabolism enzyme inducers (see above) **e.g. broccoli-like vegetables, smoking, phenobarbitone, phenytoin, rifampicin**
- *possible increase risk of extrapyramidal effects* with **dopamine antagonists e.g. metoclopramide**
- *additive hypotension with* **antihypertensives e.g. propranolol**
- *additive CNS effects* with other **CNS depressants e.g. benzodiazepines (e.g. lorazepam), phenothiazines (e.g. chlorpromazine), opioids, alcohol**

Dosing:

oral tabs/disp tabs:	2.5 to 20 mg per day as a single dose
subcut:	inj available but recommended for im use only
rectal:	not available

Syringe driver: not available

Mechanism of action: antagonises serotonin and dopamine receptors in the CNS

Notes:

- Lower potential for neurological adverse effects than conventional antipsychotics.
- Can be used in acute delirium and behavioural disturbances associated with brain tumours.

Omeprazole

Class: ulcer healing/prophylactic - proton pump inhibitor

Indications (NB some may be unlicensed): duodenal/gastric ulcer, reflux oesophagitis, dyspepsia, NSAID associated gastric and duodenal ulcer/erosion treatment

Contraindications/cautions: renal impairment

Adverse reactions: *common* headache, nausea/vomiting, diarrhoea or constipation; *less common* insomnia, dizziness, vertigo, pruritus, blood disorders, muscle/joint pain, dry mouth, agitation

Metabolism/clearance: metabolised by metabolising enzyme CYP2C19 mainly in the liver

Interactions:

- *increased clinical effect/toxicity of omeprazole* (due to increased blood concentrations) may occur with some CYP metabolising enzyme inhibitors (see above) **e.g. fluconazole, fluoxetine, ketoconazole**
- *decreased clinical effect/toxicity of omeprazole* (due to decreased blood concentrations) may occur with some CYP metabolism enzyme inducers (see above) **e.g. carbamazepine, phenytoin, rifampicin**
- *increased clinical effect/toxicity of some drugs* (due to increased blood concentrations of them) may occur with omeprazole due to metabolising enzyme inhibition by omeprazole **e.g. diazepam**
- *decreased absorption of* **itraconazole** may occur with omeprazole

Dosing:

oral:	10 to 40 mg once a day
subcut:	injection and infusion available but not usually used subcut. Doses of 40 mg in 100 mL normal saline have been given subcut over 3 hours
rectal:	not available

Syringe driver: short infusions only

Mechanism of action: inhibits gastric acid secretion via proton pump blockade

Onset: oral (antacid effect): 10 to 20 minutes

Notes:

- Omeprazole is considered the drug of choice for prophylaxis or treatment of NSAID-induced gastro-intestinal damage.
- Oral suspension can be made.

Ondansetron

Class: antiemetic - 5HT3 antagonist

Indications (NB some may be unlicensed): nausea/vomiting post chemo- or radio- therapy, post-operative nausea/vomiting, nausea/vomiting not due to above

Contraindications/cautions: hepatic impairment, subacute gastro-intestinal obstruction

Adverse reactions: *common* headache, constipation; *less common* hiccups, injection site reaction, dizziness, cardiac effects (iv usually tachycardia, chest pain, arrhythmias), sedation, convulsions

Metabolism/clearance: metabolised by metabolising enzyme CYP2D6 mainly in the liver

Interactions:

- *increased clinical effect/toxicity of ondansetron* (due to increased blood concentrations) may occur with some CYP metabolising enzyme inhibitors (see above) **e.g. bupropion, fluoxetine, paroxetine, quinine**

Dosing:

oral:	4 to 8 mg twice a day
subcut:	not usually used
rectal:	not available

Syringe driver: compatibility unknown so don't mix

Mechanism of action: acts on 5HT3 receptors in the vomiting centre in the CNS and in the gastrointestinal tract

Peak concentration: oral: 1 to 2 hours im (subcut): 30 minutes

Notes:

- May be of use in nausea and vomiting refractory to all other antiemetics.

Oxycodone

Class: analgesic - opioid

Indications: step 3 in the WHO analgesic ladder

Contraindications/cautions: severe renal failure, respiratory disease

Adverse reactions: *see morphine*

Metabolism/clearance: metabolised by metabolising enzymes CYP2D6 mainly in the liver

Interactions:

- *increased clinical effect/toxicity of oxycodone* (due to increased blood concentrations) may occur with some CYP metabolising enzyme inhibitors (see above) **e.g. bupropion, fluoxetine, paroxetine, quinine**
- *additive CNS effects* with other **CNS depressants e.g. benzodiazepines (e.g. lorazepam), phenothiazines (e.g. chlorpromazine), tricyclic antidepressants (e.g. amitriptyline), other opioids, alcohol**
- *additive respiratory depression* with **benzodiazepines (e.g. midazolam), other respiratory depressants**

Dosing: (and see notes)

oral:	immediate release	initially in opioid naïve 1 to 3 mg 4 to 6 hourly
	slow release	initially 5 mg every 12 hours
subcut:	oral:subcut	2:1
rectal:	not available	

Syringe driver: see syringe driver compatibility table

Mechanism of action: stimulates opioid receptors in the CNS and gastrointestinal tract

Onset: oral: 20 to 30 minutes

Duration: oral: (immediate release): 4 to 6 hours slow release: 12 hours

Notes:

- May be useful in opioid rotation.
- Dose conversion from oral morphine to oral oxycodone is 2:1 i.e. 10 mg oral morphine =
- 5 mg oral oxycodone because oral availability of oxycodone is twice that of morphine.
- The slow release tabs and the immediate release caps should not be opened or crushed/chewed.
- In renally impaired patients, one of oxycodone's active metabolite may accumulate.
- The combination oxycodone+naloxone modified release tablets* are designed to reduce opioid induced constipation.

*** Drugs that are either not available or not funded in New Zealand**

Pamidronate disodium

Class: bisphosphonate calcium regulator

Indications: hypercalcaemia, metastatic bone pain, Paget's disease

Contraindications/cautions: severe renal impairment, dental surgery, oral disease, ensure adequate hydration

Adverse reactions: *less common* transient flu-like symptoms, slight increase in temperature, fever, hypocalcaemia, transient bone pain, nausea, headache, osteonecrosis (particularly of jaw)

Metabolism/clearance: not metabolised, excreted by the kidneys after uptake into the bone

Interactions:

- *incompatible with calcium* containing infusion fluids

Dosing:

oral:	not available	
subcut:	zoledronic acid is usually used instead	
rectal:	not available	
iv infusion:	bone pain	90 mg every 3 to 4 weeks
	hypercalcaemia	15 to 90 mg depending on corrected calcium concentration

- rate of infusion should not exceed 60 mg/hour (20 mg/hour in renal impairment) and concentration should not exceed 90 mg/250 mL

Syringe driver: not applicable

Mechanism of action: inhibits bone resorption

Onset: hypercalcaemia: 1 to 2 days

Duration: hypercalcaemia: 2 weeks to 3 months bone pain: 3 to 4 weeks

Notes:

- 50% of patients with metastatic bone pain may be responsive.

Pantoprazole

Class: ulcer healing/prophylaxis - proton pump inhibitor

Indications: duodenal/gastric ulcer, reflux oesophagitis, dyspepsia

Contraindications/cautions: renal impairment

Adverse reactions: *common* headache, nausea/vomiting; *less common* abdominal pain, flatulence, insomnia, pruritus, dizziness

Metabolism/clearance: metabolised by metabolising enzyme CYP2C19 mainly in the liver

Interactions:

- *increased clinical effect/toxicity of pantoprazole* (due to increased blood concentrations) may occur with some CYP metabolising enzyme inhibitors (see above) **e.g. fluconazole, fluoxetine, ketoconazole**
- *decreased clinical effect/toxicity of pantoprazole* (due to decreased blood concentrations) may occur with some CYP metabolism enzyme inducers (see above) **e.g. carbamazepine, phenytoin, rifampicin**
- *decreased absorption of* **ketoconazole, itraconazole** may occur with pantoprazole

Dosing:

oral:	20 to 80 mg once a day
subcut:	inj available but not usually used subcut
rectal:	not available

Syringe driver: not usually used

Mechanism of action: inhibits gastric acid secretion via proton pump blockade.

Onset: oral (antacid effect): 2 hours

Paracetamol

Class: analgesic - non-opioid

Indications: step 1 on the WHO analgesic ladder, co-analgesic, antipyretic

Contraindications/cautions: severe hepatic impairment

Adverse reactions: *less common* rash, pancreatitis on prolonged use, liver damage in overdose (> 6 g in 24 hours) or in combination with heavy alcohol intake, nephrotoxicity

Metabolism/clearance: metabolised in the liver mainly by glucuronidation

Interactions:

- *increased toxicity of* paracetamol may occur with **alcohol**
- *increased anticoagulant effect* of **warfarin** may occur if given with concurrent paracetamol regularly for a long time so monitor INR
- *increased absorption of* paracetamol may occur with **metoclopramide and domperidone**
- *increased risk of* hepatotoxicity may occur with concurrent **carbamazepine, phenytoin**

Dosing:

oral:	500 mg to 1 g 4 to 6 hourly (max. 4 g in 24 hours)
subcut:	infusion available but large volume
rectal:	as for oral

Syringe driver: not used subcut due to high volume

Mechanism of action: thought to have a central effect on pain pathways and not anti-inflammatory

Onset: 0.5 hours

Duration: 4 hours

Notes:

- Give regularly rather than if required.
- Combination preparations are not recommended.
- Liver damage is likely to occur in overdose.
- Useful analgesic when given regularly in combination with opioids.

Phenobarbitone

Class: anticonvulsant - barbiturate

Indications (NB some may be unlicensed): seizure control, status epilepticus, pre-op anxiety,

terminal restlessness

Contraindications/cautions: acute intermittent porphyria, elderly, renal/hepatic failure

Adverse reactions: *common* drowsiness, headache; *less common* GI upset, paradoxical excitement, pain, hypocalcaemia

Metabolism/clearance: may be metabolised by metabolising enzyme CYP2C19 mainly in the liver

Interactions:

- *increased clinical effect/toxicity of phenobarbitone* (due to increased blood concentrations) may occur with some CYP metabolising enzyme inhibitors (see above) **e.g. fluconazole, fluoxetine, ketoconazole**
- *decreased clinical effect/toxicity of phenobarbitone* (due to decreased blood concentrations) may occur with some CYP metabolism enzyme inducers (see above) **e.g. phenytoin, rifampicin**
- *decreased clinical effect/toxicity of some drugs* (due to decreased blood concentrations of them) may occur with phenobarbitone due to metabolising enzyme induction by phenobarbitone **e.g. aprepitant, buspirone, carbamazepine, clonazepam, dexamethasone, diazepam, domperidone, fentanyl, itraconazole, ketoconazole, methadone, midazolam, NSAIDs (e.g. diclofenac), phenytoin, prednisone, quetiapine, triazolam, warfarin**
- *additive CNS effects* with other **CNS depressants e.g. benzodiazepines (e.g. lorazepam), phenothiazines (e.g. chlorpromazine), opioids, alcohol**

Dosing:

terminal agitation

oral:	60 to 180 mg per day
subcut:	600 to 1,200 mg/24 hours
rectal:	not available

Syringe driver: give alone and watch for irritation at injection site

Mechanism of action: depresses activity of all excitable tissue perhaps via GABA

Notes:

- Risk of respiratory depression in overdose.

Phenytoin

Class: anticonvulsant - hydantoin

Indications (NB some may be unlicensed): epilepsy, prophylaxis in neurosurgery, arrhythmias

Contraindications/cautions: low albumin

Adverse reactions: *common* gingival hyperplasia; *less common* slurred speech, confusion, dizziness, blood disorders, skin reactions, hepatitis

Metabolism/clearance: metabolised by metabolising enzyme CYP2C8/9 mainly in the liver

Interactions:

- *increased clinical effect/toxicity of phenytoin* (due to increased blood concentrations) may occur with some CYP metabolising enzyme inhibitors (see above) **e.g. fluconazole, ketoconazole, voriconazole**
- *decreased clinical effect/toxicity of phenytoin* (due to decreased blood concentrations) may occur with some CYP metabolism enzyme inducers (see above) **e.g. phenobarbitone, rifampicin**
- *decreased clinical effect/toxicity of some drugs* (due to decreased blood concentrations of them) may occur with phenytoin due to metabolising enzyme induction by phenytoin **e.g. aprepitant, buspirone, amitriptyline, carbamazepine, clonazepam, dexamethasone, diazepam, domperidone, fentanyl, itraconazole, ketoconazole, methadone, midazolam, NSAIDs (e.g. diclofenac), olanzapine, ondansetron, phenytoin, prednisone, quetiapine, triazolam, warfarin**

Dosing:

oral:	100 to 300 mg/24 hours (titrate to plasma concentrations)
subcut:	inj available but not given subcut
rectal:	not available

Syringe driver: not applicable

Mechanism of action: inhibits spread of seizure through the motor cortex possibly via sodium channels

Peak response: 7 to 10 days (if loaded 8 to 12 hours)

Notes:

- Monitor plasma concentrations.
- Small dose increases may result in large plasma concentration increases.
- If the patient has NG feeds these will affect phenytoin concentrations.

Prednisone

Class: corticosteroid - glucocorticoid

Indications (NB some may be unlicensed): allergy, asthma, rheumatic disease, inflammatory conditions, nausea/vomiting, inflammation in gastrointestinal obstruction, sweating, itch, hypercalcaemia, hiccup, pain, dyspnoea (lymphangitis), liver capsule pain, tenesmus

Contraindications/cautions: infections, gastrointestinal bleeding, diabetes, congestive heart failure, mood disorders

Adverse reactions: *common* insomnia (decrease by giving as single dose in the morning); *less common* sodium/fluid retention, GI ulceration, delayed wound healing, thinning of skin (on prolonged use), proximal muscle weakness, Cushing's syndrome, weight gain, depression, mania, delirium

Metabolism/clearance: metabolised by the metabolising enzyme CYP3A mainly in the liver

Interactions:

- *increased clinical effect/toxicity of prednisone* (due to increased blood concentrations) may occur with some CYP metabolising enzyme inhibitors (see above) **e.g. aprepitant, clarithromycin, fluconazole, fluoxetine, grapefruit juice, itraconazole, ketoconazole, valproate**
- *decreased clinical effect/toxicity of prednisone* (due to decreased blood concentrations) may occur with some CYP metabolism enzyme inducers (see above) **e.g. carbamazepine, phenobarbitone, phenytoin, rifampicin, St John's wort**
- *increased risk of GI bleed/ulceration* when given with **NSAIDs (e.g. diclofenac)**

Dosing:

oral:	10 to 100 mg usually once a day (max. 250mg/day)
subcut:	not available
rectal:	not available

Syringe driver: not available

Mechanism of action: decreases inflammatory response thought to be via induction of lipocortin, an anti-inflammatory protein

Notes:

- 0.75 mg dexamethasone has an equivalent anti-inflammatory effect to 5 mg prednisone or
- 20 mg hydrocortisone.
- On discontinuation decrease dose slowly (taper) unless the patient has been taking it for less than five days in which case dose tapering is not necessary.
- Alteration in mood not usually seen below 40 mg prednisone (6 mg dexamethasone) per day.
- Corticosteroid induced insomnia responds to benzodiazepines (e.g. temazepam).
- Corticosteroid induced mood disorder is usually depression and rarely mania.
- Metabolised to prednisolone.

Pregabalin* ....

Class: anticonvulsant

Indications (NB some may be unlicensed): neuropathic pain, adjunctive anticonvulsant

Contraindications/cautions: renal disease (reduce dose)

Adverse reactions: *common* dizziness, somnolence, blurred vision, fatigue, dry mouth, headache, tremor, constipation, nausea; *less common* weight gain, ataxia, confusion, suicidal thoughts

Metabolism/clearance: not metabolised, mainly excreted unchanged by the kidneys (fraction excreted unchanged by the kidney = 0.9) so adjust dose in renal dysfunction

Interactions:

- *additive CNS depression* with other **CNS depressants e.g. benzodiazepines (e.g. lorazepam), phenothiazines (e.g. chlorpromazine), tricyclic antidepressants (e.g. amitriptyline), opioids, alcohol**

Dosing:

oral:	neuropathic pain/epilepsy	150 to 600 mg/day in 2 divided doses (start with lower dose and increase)
subcut:	not available	
rectal:	not available	

Syringe driver: not available

Mechanism of action: may act through effects on calcium channels in the CNS and reduces release of the neurotransmitters glutamate, noradrenaline and substance P.

* **Drugs that are either not available or not funded in New Zealand**

Quetiapine

Class: antipsychotic - atypical

Indications (NB some may be unlicensed): acute and chronic psychoses including schizophrenia, manic episodes associated with bipolar disorder, nausea and vomiting, delirium

Contraindications/cautions: liver dysfunction, cardiovascular and cerebrovascular disease, hypotension, seizures, Parkinsons, DLB

Adverse reactions: *common* drowsiness, dry mouth, GI effects, tachycardia, dizziness, headache, agitation, insomnia, weight gain, dyspepsia; *less common* neuroleptic malignant syndrome, tardive dyskinesia, cholesterol changes, thyroid hormone changes, peripheral oedema, diabetes, extrapyramidal adverse effects, hepatotoxicity, blood disorders, postural hypotension, seizures, dyspnoea, sweating, rash

Metabolism/clearance: metabolised almost completely mainly in the liver by the metabolising enzyme CYP3A

Interactions:

- *increased clinical effect/toxicity of quetiapine* (due to increased blood concentrations) may occur with some CYP metabolising enzyme inhibitors (see above) **e.g. aprepitant, clarithromycin, grapefruit juice, indinavir, itraconazole, ketoconazole, nelfinavir, ritonavir, telapravir, voriconazole**
- *decreased clinical effect/toxicity of quetiapine* (due to decreased blood concentrations) may occur with some CYP metabolising enzyme inducers (see above) e.**g. carbamazepine, phenobarbitone, phenytoin, rifampicin, St John's wort**
- *possible increase risk of extrapyramidal effects* with **dopamine antagonists e.g. metoclopramide**
- *additive hypotension with* **antihypertensives e.g. propranolol** may occur
- *additive CNS effects* with other **CNS depressants e.g. benzodiazepines (e.g. lorazepam), phenothiazines (e.g. chlorpromazine), opioids, alcohol**

Dosing:

oral:	psychosis	initially 50 mg/day increasing daily to 150 to 750 mg per day in 2 divided doses
	mania	initially 100 mg/day increasing daily to 200 to 800 mg per day in 2 divided doses
	tranquillisation, sedation, antiemetic	25 to 100 mg at night
subcut:		not available
rectal:		not available

Syringe driver: not available

Mechanism of action: antagonises serotonin and dopamine receptors in the CNS

Notes:

- Lower potential for neurological adverse effects (e.g. extrapyramidal effects) than conventional antipsychotics.
- Can be used in acute delirium and behavioural disturbances associated with brain tumours.

Ranitidine

Class: ulcer healing/prophylactic - H2 antagonist

Indications (NB some may be unlicensed): duodenal/gastric ulcer, reflux oesophagitis, dyspepsia, itch, sweating

Contraindications/cautions: renal impairment

Adverse reactions: *common* diarrhoea, tiredness; *less common* blurred vision, gynaecomastia, bradycardia, tachycardia, hypotension, agitation, hallucinations, blood disorders, dizziness, headache, confusion

Metabolism/clearance: metabolised by the liver to 3 inactive metabolites which are excreted by the kidney together with 30% of the parent drug.

Interactions:

- *increased anticoagulation effect* of **warfarin** may occur
- *decreased absorption of* **itraconazole, ketoconazole** may occur
- *increased clinical effect/toxicity* of **metformin, oral midazolam** may occur

Dosing:

oral:	150 mg twice a day or 300 mg at night (reduce dose in elderly and renal impairment)
subcut:	100 to 200 mg/24 hours
rectal:	not available

Syringe driver: ?infuse alone

Mechanism of action: inhibits gastric acid secretion via histamine receptor blockade

Onset (acid suppression): oral: 10 to 20 minutes

Notes:

- Pantoprazole or omeprazole is considered the drug of choice for prophylaxis or treatment of NSAID-induced gastrointestinal damage.
- If gastrointestinal reflux is uncontrolled by pantoprazole or omeprazole, adding in a night-time dose of ranitidine may help.

Risperidone

Class: antipsychotic - atypical

Indications (NB some may be unlicensed): schizophrenia, psychosis, behavioural/psychological symptoms of dementia, conduct/behavioural disorders in mentally retarded, autism, mania in bipolar disorder, delirium

Contraindications/cautions: Parkinson's disease, DLB, epilepsy, cardiovascular/cerebrovascular disease, diabetes

Adverse reactions: *common* insomnia, anxiety, headache, extrapyramidal symptoms; *less common* drowsiness, dizziness, GI upset, sexual dysfunction, constipation, dry mouth, postural hypotension

Metabolism/clearance: metabolised by metabolising enzyme CYP3A and 2D6 mainly in the liver

Interactions:

- *increased clinical effect/toxicity of risperidone* (due to increased blood concentrations) may occur with some CYP metabolising enzyme inhibitors (see above) **e.g. aprepitant, bupropion, clarithromycin, fluoxetine, grapefruit juice, indinavir, itraconazole, ketoconazole, nelfinavir, paroxetine, quinine, ritonavir, telapravir, voriconazole**
- *decreased clinical effect/toxicity of risperidone* (due to decreased blood concentrations) may occur with some CYP metabolism enzyme inducers (see above) **e.g. carbamazepine, phenobarbitone, phenytoin, rifampicin, St John's wort**
- *possible increased risk of extrapyramidal effects* with **dopamine antagonists e.g. metoclopramide**
- *additive hypotension may* occur with **antihypertensives e.g. enalapril**
- *additive CNS effects* with other **CNS depressants e.g. benzodiazepines (e.g. lorazepam), phenothiazines (e.g. chlorpromazine), opioids, alcohol**

Dosing:

oral:	schizophrenia	initially 2 mg/day increasing to 4 to 6 mg/day (max 16 mg/day)
	bipolar mania	initially 2 mg/day increasing to 2 to 6 mg/day
	dementia	initially 0.25 mg twice a day increasing to a max. of 1 mg twice a day
	psychosis	0.5 to 4 mg twice a day
subcut/rectal:		not available

Syringe driver: not available

Mechanism of action: antagonises serotonin and dopamine receptors in the CNS

Onset: psychosis: 1 to 2 weeks

Notes:

- Lower potential for neurological adverse effects e.g. extrapyramidal effects than conventional antipsychotics.
- Increasingly used in acute delirium and behavioural disturbances associated with brain tumours.
- At high dose (> 6 to 8 mg a day) or in the cerebrally compromised patient extrapyramidal side effects may occur.

Senna

Class: laxative - stimulant

Indications: constipation

Contraindications/cautions: acute abdominal pain, intestinal obstruction

Adverse reactions: *common* abdominal cramps, diarrhoea, perianal irritation; *less common* atonic colon (with prolonged use), hypokalaemia, discolouration of urine (brown or pink)

Metabolism/clearance: not absorbed to a great extent

Interactions:

- *decreased antispasmodic effects* of **antispasmodics e.g. hyoscine butylbromide** may occur

Dosing:

oral:	2 to 4 tabs (14 to 28 mg) at night with docusate 1 to 2 tabs at night (max. 4 tabs)
subcut:	not available
rectal:	not available

Syringe driver: not available

Mechanism of action: stimulates colonic activity via nerves in the intestinal mucosa. May also have stool softening properties.

Onset: 6 to 12 hours

Notes:

- May be useful in opioid induced constipation.

continued

Spironolactone

Class: diuretic - aldosterone antagonist, potassium sparing

Indications (NB some may be unlicensed): oedema, hypertension, congestive heart failure, hirsutism, hyperaldosteronism, malignant ascites

Contraindications/cautions: moderate/severe renal dysfunction, hyperkalaemia, hyponatraemia

Adverse reactions: *common* GI upset, drowsiness, hyperkalaemia; *less common* rashes, headache, confusion, impotence, gynaecomastia, hyponatraemia

Metabolism/clearance: metabolised in liver to active metabolites which are excreted partially by the kidneys

Interactions:

- *increased risk of hyperkalaemia* with **NSAIDs (e.g. diclofenac), ACE inhibitors (e.g. cilazapril, quinapril), potassium** supplements
- *increased clinical effect/toxicity* of **digoxin** may occur via increased digoxin concentrations

Dosing:

oral:	malignant ascites	100 to 200 mg once a day (max. 400 mg daily)
subcut/rectal		not available

Syringe driver: not available

Mechanism of Action: inhibits aldosterone causing naturesis and potassium retention

Peak response: aldosterone antagonism: 6 to 8 hours
reduced ascites: 10 to 25 days

Notes:

- Paracentesis may be necessary in malignant ascites.
- Monitor body weight and renal function.

Tramadol

Class: analgesic - opioid (with extra effect on inhibitory pain pathways)

Indications: step 2 on the WHO analgesic ladder

Contraindications/cautions: epilepsy, drug abuse, respiratory depression

Adverse reactions: *common* nausea, vomiting, diarrhoea, sweating (dose related); *less common* dry mouth, sedation, headache, hypertension, confusion

Metabolism/clearance: metabolised by metabolising enzyme CYP2D6 mainly in the liver to an active metabolite

Interactions:

- *increased clinical effect/toxicity of tramadol* (due to increased blood concentrations) may occur with some CYP metabolising enzyme inhibitors (see above) **e.g. bupropion, fluoxetine, paroxetine, quinine**
- *additive CNS effects* with other **CNS depressants e.g. benzodiazepines (e.g. lorazepam), phenothiazines (e.g. chlorpromazine), other opioids, alcohol**
- *additive risk of serotonin syndrome* (potentially fatal syndrome - symptoms include sweating, diarrhoea, confusion) with other serotonergic drugs **e.g. amitriptyline, carbamazepine, citalopram, fluoxetine, lithium, paroxetine**
- *decreases seizure threshold* so may interact with **anticonvulsants e.g. carbamazepine**

Dosing:

oral:	normal release	50 to 100 mg 4 hourly (max. 400 mg/24 hours)
	slow release	100 to 200 mg twice a day
subcut:		up to 600 mg/24 hours
rectal:		not available

Syringe driver: give separately as compatibility as yet unknown

Mechanism of action: stimulates mu opioid receptors in CNS and gastrointestinal tract and also affects noradrenaline and serotonin in descending spinal inhibitory pain pathways

Peak effect: oral (normal release): 0.5 to 1 hour

Duration: oral (normal release): 3 to 7 hours

Notes:

- Place in palliative therapy still to be established.
- May be useful in patients who are constipated on codeine as it is less constipating generally.
- Start with low dose to minimise adverse effects.
- It is not a controlled drug.

Tranexamic acid

Class: antifibrinolytic, haemostatic

Indications: haemorrhage - surface bleeding from tumours, nose and other organs

Contraindications/cautions: active clotting, urinary tract bleeds (as clots may rarely form in the urinary tract), renal dysfunction, subarachnoid haemorrhage, acquired defective colour vision

Adverse reactions: *common* GI upset; *less common* dizziness (iv), thrombocytopenia, headache, restlessness, impaired colour vision

Interactions:

- *decreased clinical effect of anticoagulants* **e.g. warfarin** may occur with tranexamic acid

Dosing:

haemorrhage

oral:	1 to 1.5 g 3 to 4 times a day
subcut:	not used
rectal:	the injection has been used rectally for rectal bleeding
topical:	the injection has been used topically on bleeding wounds
iv:	0.5 to 1 g 2 to 3 times a day

Syringe driver: not applicable

Mechanism of action: interacts with plasminogen to cause antifibrinolysis

Peak effect: 3 hours

Notes:

- Tablets are large and many patients may have difficulty swallowing them.

Valproate (sodium)

Class: anticonvulsant, antipsychotic

Indications (NB some may be unlicensed): epilepsy, bipolar disease, neuropathic pain

Contraindications/cautions: liver dysfunction

Adverse reactions: *common* GI upset, tremor; *less common* thrombocytopenia, sedation, transient hair loss, hepatotoxicity

Metabolism/clearance: may be metabolised by CYP metabolising enzymes family mainly in the liver

Interactions:

- *increased clinical effect/toxicity of some drugs* (due to increased blood concentrations of them) may occur variably with valproate due to metabolising enzyme inhibition by valproate **e.g. amitriptyline, carbamazepine, citalopram, NSAIDs (e.g. diclofenac), pantoprazole, phenobarbitone, phenytoin**
- *decreased clinical effect/toxicity of valproate* (due to decreased blood concentrations) may occur with some CYP metabolism enzyme inducers **e.g. carbamazepine**

Dosing:

neuropathic pain

oral:	200 to 1,000 mg twice a day (max. 2,500 mg per day, start low)
subcut:	available in injectable form, not usually used
rectal:	not available

Syringe driver: not applicable

Mechanism of action: pain - as for carbamazepine

Peak effect: not known but peak concentrations reached in 4 to 8 hours

Notes:

- Co-analgesic often used with opioids in the treatment of neuropathic pain although gabapentin or pregabalin have become common alternatives.
- May be used in neuropathic pain when tricyclic antidepressants have failed or in combination with tricyclic antidepressants.
- When switching from carbamazepine to valproate watch for toxicity from other drugs as carbamazepine induces the metabolism of several drugs while valproate inhibits the metabolism of several drugs.
- Don't discontinue abruptly as risk of rebound seizures.
- Therapeutic drug monitoring is usually available but is of limited value.
- Monitor LFTs.

Venlafaxine

Class: antidepressant - bicyclic, SNRI

Indications (NB some may be unlicensed): depression, anxiety disorders, ?neuropathic pain, hot flushes

Contraindications/cautions: renal/hepatic failure, volume depletion, epilepsy, mania, heart disease

Adverse reactions: *common* nervousness, headache, fatigue, blood pressure changes, dizziness, dry mouth, insomnia, drowsiness, weight gain or loss, GI effects, sexual dysfunction, sweating, weakness, prolongation of the QT interval; *less common* tremor, mania, anxiety, palpitations, heart failure, loss of consciousness, seizures, blood disorders, hepatitis, arrhythmias, neuroleptic malignant syndrome, pancreatitis, extrapyramidal adverse effects, hypercholesteraemia

Metabolism/clearance: metabolised by metabolising enzyme CYP2D6 mainly in the liver to active metabolites. Some venlafaxine and some of its metabolites are excreted by the kidneys.

Interactions:

- *increased clinical effect/toxicity of venlafaxine* (due to increased blood concentrations) may occur with some CYP metabolising enzyme inhibitors (see above) **e.g. bupropion, fluoxetine, paroxetine, quinine**
- *increased clinical effect/toxicity of some drugs* (due to increased blood concentrations of them) may occur with venlafaxine due to metabolising enzyme inhibition **e.g. codeine** (effect may be decreased due to lack of metabolism to morphine), **nortriptyline**
- *increased risk of serotonin syndrome* with MAOIs **e.g. phenelzine** so avoid venlafaxine within 2 weeks of MAOI therapy
- *increased risk of prolonged QT interval* with other drugs that prolong the interval **e.g. haloperidol**

Dosing:

oral:	modified release	37.5 to 375 mg once a day
subcut:		not available
rectal:		not available

Syringe driver: not available

Mechanism of action: inhibits reuptake of serotonin (at high dose), noradrenaline and dopamine in the CNS

Notes:

- Effectiveness in neuropathic pain is yet to be evaluated.

Warfarin

Class: anticoagulant

Indications: thrombotic disorders prophylaxis

Contraindications/cautions: potential haemorrhagic conditions

Adverse reactions: *common* bleeding; *less common* hair loss; *rare* purple toe syndrome

Metabolism/clearance: metabolised by the metabolising enzymes CYP 1A2, 2C19 and 2C9 mainly in the liver

Interactions:

- *increased clinical effect/toxicity of warfarin* (due to increased blood concentrations) may occur with some CYP metabolising enzyme inhibitors (see above) **e.g. ciprofloxacin, fluconazole, fluoxetine, ketoconazole, pantoprazole**
- *decreased clinical effect/toxicity of warfarin* (due to decreased blood concentrations) may occur with some CYP metabolism enzyme inducers (see above) **e.g. broccoli like vegetables, carbamazepine, phenobarbitone, phenytoin, rifampicin, smoking**
- *increased risk of bleeding* with **aspirin, SSRIs (e.g. fluoxetine), NSAIDs (e.g. diclofenac)**
- *increased clinical effect of warfarin* may occur with **paracetamol**
- *decreased clinical effect of warfarin* may occur with **phytomenadione (vitamin K) and foods rich in vitamin K**

NB Any changes in drug therapy should be accompanied by an INR check.

Dosing:

oral:	adjusted to INR (see below)
subcut:	not available
rectal:	not available

Syringe driver: not available

Mechanism of action: interferes with vitamin K synthesis

Notes:

- A low molecular weight heparin e.g. enoxaparin may be better tolerated.
- Different brands are not proven to be equivalent.

continued

Treatment in DVT and PE	INR	Duration
Pre and perioperative anticoagulation	1.5 to 2.0	days
Treatment of calf DVT	2.0 to 3.0	4 - 6 weeks
Treatment of provoked DVT	2.0 to 3.0	12 - 26 weeks
Treatment of provoked PE or massive DVT	2.0 to 3.0	26 - 52 weeks
Treatment of unprovoked PE or DVT	2.0 to 3.0	life long
Treatment of recurrent PE or DVT[#]	3.0 to 4.0	life long
Atrial Fibrillation	2.0 to 3.0	life long
Mechanical heart valves		
Aortic valve replacement	2.0 to 2.5	life long
Mitral valve replacement	2.5 to 3.0	life long
Arterial disease	3.0 to 4.0	life long

#recurrence despite prothrombin ratio between 2 and 3

Table from Management Guidelines for Common Medical Conditions, 15th Edition 2013, Canterbury District Health Board, New Zealand

Zoledronic acid

Class: bisphosphonate - calcium regulator

Indications (NB some may be unlicensed): osteoporosis treatment and prevention, Paget's disease, prevention of further fracture after hip fracture, hypercalcaemia of malignancy, bone metastases

Contraindications/cautions: renal or hepatic impairment, cardiac impairment, hypocalcaemic, phosphataemic or magnesaemic patients, administration with diuretics and other nephrotoxic drugs

Adverse reactions: *common* hypotension, fatigue, fever and other flu-like symptoms, GI upset (nausea), rash, chest pain, renal toxicity; *less common* anxiety, insomnia, hypocalcaemia, hypophosphataemia and hypomagnesaemia, sore mouth/throat, eye irritation, conjunctivitis

Metabolism/clearance: excreted unchanged by the kidneys and not metabolised

Interactions:

- *additive risk of* renal toxicity with other **nephrotoxic drugs e.g. frusemide, thalidomide**

Dosing:

oral:	not available	
subcut:	not usual but has been tried	
rectal:	not available	
iv infusion:	hypercalcaemia	4 mg iv infused over 15 mins
	bone met pain	4mg iv as above every 3 to 4 weeks

Syringe driver: not applicable

Mechanism of action: inhibits bone resorption

Onset: hypercalcaemia: 2 to 3 days

Duration: hypercalcaemia: 32 to 39 days
bone pain: 4 to 6 weeks

Notes:

- Patients must be adequately hydrated before administration of zoledronic acid, especially the elderly and those on diuretics
- Renal impairment has been noted after a single administration of the drug. Routinely check serum creatinine clearance pre-administration and cease zoledronic acid if creatinine this is becoming impaired.
- Osteonecrosis of the jaw has been noted predominantly in adults receiving bisphosphonate infusions
- Occasionally severe muscle, bone and joint pain is experienced after infusion, mostly this is relieved after stopping treatment

Syringe drivers

A syringe driver is a battery-operated pump which administers drugs subcutaneously- consult a specialist for information on the pump used in your area and how to use it. Many of the drugs administered via the syringe driver are not licensed for subcutaneous use and the responsibility for their use lies with the prescriber

Indications

- severe nausea and/or vomiting
- dysphagia
- severe oral lesions
- non - absorption of oral medication
- unconscious or sedated patient

Diluent

- most drugs and drug combinations used in a syringe driver need to be made up to a certain number of millimetres or volume with a diluent
- generally water for injection is currently used
- some drugs, however must be diluted with a specified diluent e.g. levomepromazine (methotrimeprazine) in normal saline
- both water for injection and normal saline have advantages and disadvantages:
  - water for injection
    - > has few ions present and therefore is less likely to cause precipitation of drugs out of solution
    - > BUT may be more irritant to subcutaneous tissue
  - normal saline
    - > contains ions and so is more likely to cause precipitation of drugs
    - > BUT may be more like interstitial fluid and therefore less irritant to subcutaneous tissue

Compatibility

- often several drugs are combined in one syringe
- little work has been done on the compatibility of drugs in syringe drivers (see chart)
- examination of the drugs in the syringe may reveal visual incompatibility, e.g. precipitation BUT non-visual chemical reactions may be occurring leading to the inactivation of one or more of the drugs or the production of potentially toxic compounds
- only combine drugs that are absolutely essential - if there is any doubt, consultation with a drug information pharmacist will guide practice
- avoid combining more than three drugs in one syringe
- consider the use of more than one syringe driver when more than three drugs need to be given via this route or if there are concerns about compatibility

The following drugs should never be given subcutaneously
DIAZEPAM, PROCHLORPERAZINE, CHLORPROMAZINE

Syringe Driver Compatibilty Table

Compatibility of drugs for use in syringe drivers over 24 hours of subcutaneous infusions	clonazepam	cyclizine	dexamethasone	fentanyl	glycopyrrolate	haloperidol	hydromorphone
clonazepam	-	SI	Y	?	Y	Y	?
cyclizine	SI	-	SI	SI	Y	Y	?
dexamethasone	Y	SI	-	?	?	SI	?
fentanyl	?	SI	?	-	Y	Y	-
glycopyrrolate	Y	Y	?	Y	-	Y	Y
haloperidol	Y	Y	SI	Y	Y	-	Y
hydromorphone	?	?	?	-	Y	Y	-
hyoscine butyl bromide (Buscopan™)	Y	SI	Y	Y	?	Y	Y
hyoscine hydrobromide	Y	Y	Y	Y	NA	Y	Y
ketamine	Y	?	Y	Y	Y	Y	?
methotrimeprazine/ levomepromazine (Nozinan™)	Y	Y	SI	Y	Y	Y	Y
methadone	Y	?	Y	?	Y	Y	?
metoclopramide	Y	Y	Y	Y	Y	Y	
midazolam	Y	SI	SI	Y	Y	Y	Y
morphine sulphate (normal strengths)	Y	Y	Y	?	Y	Y	-
morphine tartrate (high strengths)	Y	Y	Y	?	?	SI	-
octreotide	Y	SI	SI	Y	Y	Y	?
ondansetron	?	Y	Y	Y	Y	Y	?
oxycodone	Y	SI	Y	?	Y	Y	-
phenobarbitone	?	?	?	Y	N	?	?

Combinations that have been used

Y = compatible	morphine+clonazepam+cyclizine (morphine sulphate and tartrate)
N = incompatible	morphine+clonazepam+dexamethasone (morphine sulphate and tartrate)
SI = sometimes incompatible (usually at higher concentrations)	morphine+clonazepam+haloperidol (morphine sulphate and tartrate)
NA = not usually used together	morphine+clonazepam+ketamine (morphine sulphate and tartrate)
? = unknown	morphine+clonazepam+metoclopramide (morphine sulphate Y, tartrate SI)

Info from:
1) The Palliative Care Handbook 7TH Edition 2014 – 24 hour syringe driver compatibility for subcutaneous administration table. 2) Palliative Medicine Handbook on line at http://book.pallcare.info/index.php
3) Compatibility of syringe driver admixtures for continuous subcutaneous infusions, Department of Pharmacy,

Diluent: water is recommended for all infusions except ketamine, octreotide, ondansetron and levomepromazine where sodium chloride 0.9% should be used although in combinations consider water.

hyoscine butyl bromide(Buscopan™)	hyoscine hydrobromide	ketamine	methotrimeprazine/ levomepromazine (Nozinan™)	methadone	metoclopramide	midazolam	morphine sulphate (normal strengths)	morphine tartrate (high strengths)	octreotide	ondansetron	oxycodone	phenobarbitone
Y	Y	Y	Y	Y	Y	Y	Y	Y	Y	?	Y	?
SI	Y	?	Y	?	Y	SI	Y	Y	SI	Y	SI	?
Y	Y	Y	SI	Y	Y	SI	Y	Y	SI	Y	Y	?
Y	Y	Y	Y	?	Y	Y	?	?	Y	Y	?	Y
?	NA	Y	Y	Y	Y	Y	Y	?	Y	Y	Y	N
Y	Y	Y	Y	Y	Y	Y	Y	SI	Y	Y	Y	?
Y	Y	?	Y	?	-	Y	-	-	?	?	-	?
-	NA	Y	Y	?	Y	Y	Y	?	Y	Y	Y	?
NA	-	Y	Y	Y	Y	Y	Y	Y	Y	Y	Y	?
Y	Y	-	Y	?	Y	Y	Y	Y	Y	Y	Y	?
Y	Y	Y	-	Y	Y	Y	Y	Y	SI	Y	Y	?
?	Y	?	Y	-	Y	Y	?	?	?	?	?	N
Y	Y	Y	Y	Y	-	Y	Y	Y	Y	Y	Y	?
Y	Y	Y	Y	Y	Y	-	Y	Y	Y	Y	Y	?
Y	Y	Y	Y	?	Y	Y	-	NA	Y	Y	NA	?
?	Y	Y	Y	?	Y	Y	NA	-	?	Y	NA	Y
Y	Y	Y	SI	?	Y	Y	Y	?	-	Y	Y	?
Y	Y	Y	Y	?	Y	Y	Y	Y	Y	-	Y	?
Y	Y	Y	Y	?	Y	Y	NA	NA	Y	Y	-	?
?	?	?	?	N	?	?	?	Y	?	?	?	-

morphine+cyclizine+dexamethasone (morphine sulphate and tartrate)	morphine+dexamethasone+haloperidol (morphine sulphate and tartrate)
morphine+cyclizine+haloperidol (morphine sulphate and tartrate)	morphine+dexamethasone+hyoscine hydrobromide (morphine sulphate and tartrate)
morphine+cyclizine+hyoscine butyl bromide (morphine sulphate, tartrate SI)	morphine+dexamethasone+metoclopramide (morphine sulphate and tartrate)
morphine+cyclizine+metoclopramide (morphine sulphate and tartrate)	morphine+dexamethasone+midazolam (morphine sulphate SI, tartrate SI)
morphine+cyclizine+midazolam (morphine sulphate and tartrate)	morphine+dexamethasone+haloperidol (morphine sulphate and tartrate)

Auckland District Health Board 2002 4) Palliative Care Formulary on line at www.palliativedrugs.co.uk
5) Gardiner P R Compatibility of an injectable oxycodone formulation with typical diluents, syringes, tubings, infusion bags and drugs for potential co-administration. Hospital Pharmacist 2003; 10: 354-61

Useful resources

Standardised Mini-Mental State Examination (SMMSE)
https://www.ihpa.gov.au/what-we-do/standardised-mini-mental-state-examination-smmse

The Montreal Cognitive Assessment (MoCA)
http://www.mocatest.org/

Cancer pain management guidelines (Australia)
http://wiki.cancer.org.au/australia/Guidelines:Cancer_pain_management

International Association for the Study of Pain (IASP)
https://www.iasp-pain.org/

Abbey Pain Scale
https://www.apsoc.org.au/PDF/Publications/Abbey_Pain_Scale.pdf

Electronic Pain Assessment Tool (PainChek)
http://www.painchek.com/

Caresearch – palliative care knowledge network
http://www.caresearch.com.au/

Palliativedrugs.com
http://www.palliativedrugs.com/

The Palliative Care Bridge
www.palliativecarebridge.com.au/

Palliative Care Matters
http://www.pallcare.info/

National Cancer Institute
http://www.cancer.gov/

Macmillan Cancer Support
http://www.macmillan.org.uk/

Spirituality
https://smhs.gwu.edu/gwish/global-network

Dying
https://www.dyingmatters.org/

Advance care planning
https://www.advancecareplanning.org.au/
http://www.advancecareplanning.org.nz/
https://www.caresearch.com.au/caresearch/tabid/4110/Default.aspx

The Australian Commission on Safety and Quality in Health Care has released a national consensus statement "Essential elements for safe and high-quality end-of-life care in acute hospitals". Available at http://www.safetyandquality.gov.au/publications/national-consensus-statement-essential-elements-for-safe-high-quality-end-of-life-care/

Dietitians Association of Australia (2009) Evidence based Practice Guidelines for the Nutritional Management of Malnutrition in Adult Patients Across the Continuum of Care. Nutrition & Dietetics, 66 (suppl. 3): S4-S10

Palliative Care Victoria pamphlet 'About Nutrition in Palliative Care' https://www.pcvlibrary.asn.au/download/attachments/688132/Nutrition.pdf?version=1

Diabetes management at end of life
https://www.diabetes.org.uk/professionals/position-statements-reports/diagnosis-ongoing-management-monitoring/end-of-life-care

Dementia
HammondCare's Dementia Centre https://www.dementiacentre.com
Dementia Support Australia https://www.dementia.com.au
Alzheimer's Disease International https://www.alz.co.uk/

Further reading

Books

Ahmedzai S, Baldwin DR, Currow DC (eds) (2012) *Oxford Textbook - Supportive care in respiratory disease.* Oxford University Press, Oxford

Australian Wound Management Association. *Pan Pacific Clinical Practice Guideline for the Prevention and Management of Pressure Injury.* Cambridge Media Osborne Park, WA: 2012.

Ayonide OT et al (2000) The rediscovery of methadone for cancer pain management. *Med J Aust. 2000 173:536-540*

Cherny N, Fallon M, Kassa S, Portenoy R, Currow, D (eds) (2015). Oxford Textbook of Palliative Medicine (5th ed). Oxford; Oxford University Press.

Chochinov HM, Brietbart W (eds) (2012) *Handbook of Psychiatry in Palliative Medicine.* Oxford; Oxford University Press

Chochinov HM (2012) *Dignity Therapy; final words for final days*. Oxford; Oxford University Press

Farrell B (2010) *Oxford Textbook of Palliative Nursing* (3rd ed) Oxford; Oxford University Press

Faull C, Blankley K (2015) *Palliative Care* (2nd ed) Oxford; Oxford University Press

Goldman A, Hain R, Liben S (eds) (2015) *Oxford Textbook of Palliative Care for Children*. Oxford; Oxford University Press

Lipowski ZJ (1980) *Delirium: acute brain failure in man.* Springfield; Charles C Thomas

Lishman WA (1998) *Organic Psychiatry: the psychological consequences of cerebral disorder.* 3rd Edition. Oxford; Blackwell

Lloyd-Williams M (ed) (2008) *Psychosocial issues in palliative care* (2nd ed). Oxford; Oxford University Press

Lucas C (2009) *Oxford Handbook of Palliative Care* (2nd ed) Oxford; Oxford University Press

Maddocks I, Brew B, Waddy H, Williams I (2006) *Palliative Neurology.* Cambridge; Cambridge University Press

Macleod AD (2011) *The Psychiatry of Palliative Medicine – The dying mind* (2nd ed) Oxford; Radcliffe Publishing

Mitchell G (2007) *Palliative Care: A patient-centered approach*. Oxford; Radcliffe Health

Morgan-Jones P, Colombage E, McIntosh D, Ellis P (2014) *Don't give me eggs that bounce: 118 cracking recipes for people with Alzheimer's*. Sydney; HammondCare Media

Morgan-Jones P, Greedy L, Ellis P, McIntosh D (2016) *It's all about the food not the fork! 107 easy to eat meals in a mouthful.* Sydney; HammondCare Media

Morgan-Jones P, MacLeod RD, Ellis P, Lynch J (2018) *Lobster for Josino: Fabulous food for our final days.* Sydney; HammondCare Media

Palliative Care Expert Group (2010) *Therapuetic Guidelines: palliative care. Version 3.* Melbourne: Therapeutic Guidelines Limited.

Read S (2006) *Palliative care for people with learning disabilities.* London; Quay Books.

Sandler J, Dare C, Holder A (1972) *The Patient and the Analyst: The basis of the psychoanalytic process.* New York; International Universities Press

Thomas, B, Bishop, J (2009) *Manual of dietetic practice* 4th edition, Oxford; Blackwell

Twycross, R.G., Wilcock A, Howard P. (2015) *PCF5: Palliative care formulary* (5th ed.) www.palliativedrugs.com. Oxford, New York; Radcliffe Publishing

Voltz R, Bernat JL, Borasio GD et al. (eds) (2004) *Palliative Care in Neurology.* Oxford; Oxford University Press

Journal articles

American Psychiatric Association Guidelines (2004) Practice Guideline for the treatment of patients with acute stress disorder and posttraumatic stress disorder. *American Journal of Psychiatry.* 161:11, Supplement, 3-23

Auret K, Schug SA (2013) Pain management for the cancer patient –Current practice and future developments. *Best Practice & Research Clinical Anaesthesiology* 27: 545–561

Australian Wound Management Association. (2012) *Pan Pacific Clinical Practice Guideline for the Prevention and Management of Pressure Injury.* Cambridge Media Osborne Park, WA

Broadbent A, Khor K, Heaney A (2003) Palliation and chronic renal failure: opioid and other palliative medications – dosage guidelines. *Progress in Palliative Care.* DOI 10.1179/096992603225002627

Calman KC (1984) Quality of life in cancer patients: an hypothesis. *Journal of Medical Ethics* 10: 124-27

Clayton JM, Hancock KM, Butow PN, Tattersall M, Currow DC (2007) Clinical practice guidelines for communicating prognosis and end-of-life issues with adults in the advanced stages of a life-limiting illness, and their caregivers. *Medical Journal of Australia* 186 (12); S77-108

Chochinov HM (2000) Psychiatry and terminal illness. *Canadian Journal of Psychiatry.* 45:143-150

Cochinov H, Wilson K, Enns M, et al. (1997) "Are you depressed?" Screening for depression in the terminally ill. *American Journal of Psychiatry.* 151:674-676

Dein S (2005) Working with the patient who is in denial. European Journal of Palliative Care. 12:251-253

Egan R, MacLeod R, Jaye C, McGee R, Baxter J, Herbison P (2011) What is spirituality? Evidence from a New Zealand hospice study. *Mortality,* 16(4): 307-324

Finnerup, D et al (2015) Pharmacotherapy for neuropathic pain in adults:

a systematic review and meta-analysis *Lancet Neurology.* 162–73

Goodarzi Z et al (2017) Depression case finding in individuals with dementia: A systematic review and meta-analysis. *Journal of the American Geriatrics Society.* 65:937-948

Grant L, Murray S A, Sheik A (2010) Spiritual dimensions of dying in pluralist societies. *British Medical Journal.* 341:c4859

Higgs CMB Vella-Brincat J (1995) Withdrawal with transdermal fentanyl. *Journal of Pain and Symptom Management.* 10(1): 4-5

Kissane DW, Clarke DM, Street AF (2001) Demoralisation syndrome - a relevant psychiatric diagnosis for palliative care. *Journal of Palliative Care.* 17:12-21

Krajnik M, & Zylicz Z (2001) Understanding pruritus in systemic disease. *Journal of Pain and Symptom Management.* 21(2), 151-168.

Kristjanson LJ, Aoun SM, & Oldham L (2006) Palliative care and support for people with neurodegenerative conditions and their carers. *International Journal of Palliative Nursing.* 12(8): 368-377

Lawler PG. (2002) The panorama of opioid-related cognitive dysfunction in patients with cancer: a critical literature appraisal. *Cancer.* 94:1836-1853

Lim K-M, Smith M, Ortiz V (2001) Culture and Psychopharmacology. *Psychiatry Clinics of North America.* 24:523-538

Lim LC, Rosenthal MA, Maartens N, et al. (2004) Management of brain metastases: review. *Internal Medicine Journal.* 34:270-278

Littlejohn C, Baldacchino A, Bannister J. (2004) Chronic non-cancer pain and opioid dependence. *Journal of the Royal Society of Medicine.* 97:62-65

Macleod AD (2002) Neurogenic pulmonary edema in palliative care. *Journal of Pain and Symptom Management.* 23(2):154-156

Macleod AD (1998) Methylphenidate in terminal depression. *Journal of Pain and Symptom Management.* 16(3):193-198

Macleod AD (2006) Delirium: the clinical concept. *Palliative and Supportive Care.* 4:305-12

Macleod AD, Vella-Brincat J, Frampton C (2003) Swallowing capsules *Palliative Medicine.* 17(6):559

MacLeod RD (2005) Dyspnoea – management: psychosocial therapies in Ahmedzai S, Muers M (eds) Oxford Textbook – *Supportive care in respiratory disease.* Oxford University Press, Oxford p227-237

MacLeod R, Rowland P (2008) Online Resource (CD and Web), *Diagnostic Toolkit: Pain Assessment Made Easy,* Goodfellow Unit, University of Auckland, http://pame.auckland.ac.nz/

Mancini AD, Griffin P, Bonanno GA. (2012) Recent trends in the treatment of prolonged grief. *Current Opinions in Psychiatry.* 25:46-51

Milton J. (2006) The impact of complementary therapy on mainstream practice. *International Journal of Palliative Nursing,* 12(3); 121-122

Moller H-J (1999) Effectiveness and safety of benzodiazepines. *Journal of Clinical Psychopharmacology* 19(Suppl 2):2S-11S

Noble H, & Kelly D (2006) Supportive and palliative care in end stage renal failure: the need for further research. *International Journal of Palliative Nursing,* 12(8), 362-364, 366-367

Puchalski C, Ferrell B, Virani R, Otis-Green S, Baird P, Bull J, et al. (2009) Improving the quality of spiritual care as a dimension of palliative care: the report of the Consensus Conference. *Journal of Palliative Medicine.* (10):885-904

Qaseem A et al (2015) Risk Assessment and Prevention of Pressure Ulcers: A Clinical Practice Guideline From the American College of Physicians *Ann Intern Med.* 2015;162:359-369. doi:10.7326/M14-1567 www.annals.org

Rhee C, Broadbent AM (2007) Palliation and liver failure: palliative medications dosage guideline. *Journal of Palliative Medicine.* 10:3; 677-685

Seden K, Dickinson L, Khoo S, Back D (2010) Grapefruit-drug interactions *Drugs*, 70, 18, 2373-2407

Senthil, K.P., Krishna, P., Kamalaksha, S. & Manisha, R. 2014, "Role of Nutrition and Dietetics in Palliative Cancer Care: A Special Perspective", *International Journal of Food, Nutrition and Dietetics*, vol. 2, no. 1, pp. 41-44.

Sirios F. (2003) Steroid psychosis: a review. *General Hospital Psychiatry* 25:27-33

Skevington SM, Pilaar M, Routh D, MacLeod RD (1997) On the Language of Breathlessness. *Psychology and Health* 12: 677-689

Toombs J (2008) Oral methadone dosing for chronic pain. A practitioner's guide. *Pain Treatment Topics* March:1-12

Smith HS. (2003) Management of hiccups in the palliative care population. *American Journal of Hospice and Palliative Care*, 20(2); 149-154

Solano JP, Gomes B, & Higginson I. (2006) A comparison of symptom prevalence in far advanced cancer, AIDS, heart disease, chronic obstructive pulmonary disease and renal disease. *Journal of Pain and Symptom Management,* 31(1), 58-69

Twycross R, Greaves MW, Handwerker H, et al. (2003) Itch: scratching more than the surface. *Quarterly Journal of Medicine* 96:7-26

Vella-Brincat J, Macleod AD (2007) Adverse effects of opioids on the central nervous systems of palliative care patients. *Journal of Pain and Palliative Care Pharmacotherapy.* 21(1): 15-25

Vella-Brincat J, Macleod AD (2004) Haloperidol in palliative care. *Palliative Medicine.* 18(3): 195-201

William L, MacLeod RD (2008) Therapy in Practice: Management of Breakthrough Pain in Patients with Cancer. *Drugs* 68(7): 913-924

Zhukovsky D (2002) Fever and sweats in the patient with advanced cancer. *Hematology/Oncology Clinics of North America,* 16(3): 579-588

Notes

Notes

Notes

Notes

ISBN 978-0-6482415-7-7